Sharon Welch's
KNITTED TOYS

SHARON WELCH'S
KNITTED TOYS

HAMLYN

THIS BOOK IS FOR MY MOTHER, WHO TAUGHT ME TO KNIT WHEN I WAS FOUR YEARS OLD.

Editorial: SALLY HARDING, JANE McINTOSH

Design: LISA TAI

Special photography: RON KELLY

Styling: GILLIE SPARGO

Illustrations: VICKY EMPTAGE

Special acknowledgements:
Photograph on page 7 by Sue Atkinson
Teddy bear in front cover photograph manufactured by Steiff

First published in Great Britain in 1993 by Hamlyn,
an imprint of Reed Consumer Books Ltd,
Michelin House, 81 Fulham Road, London SW3 6RB
and Auckland, Melbourne, Singapore and Toronto

ISBN 0 600 57730 9

A CIP catalogue record for this book is available at the British Library

Produced by Mandarin Offset
Printed and bound in Hong Kong

CONTENTS

INTRODUCTION

Knitted toys are ideal for young children as they are soft, comforting and washable. The toys included here are very simple to make and will give hours of playtime fun. Some parts of the toy can be knitted in the child's favourite colours.

Each toy has its own personal character and by changing facial expressions, clothes or colours, new characters will develop, giving a never-ending list of things to make. Most of the toys featured in this book are made from double knitting yarn and require 100 g of yarn or less.

TOY SAFETY

All toys should be stuffed with non-flammable, washable stuffing. Always make sure that the toy is safe for the child you are giving it to. Children under three years of age should not be given any toy that has beads or buttons, loose hair or any piece which may be easily swallowed if it becomes detached from the toy. When making toys, ensure that all the pieces are securely sewn together and fastened firmly in place as instructed.

Remember that very small toys are not suitable for babies and toddlers, because they could present a choking hazard.

CHOOSING YARN

Always use machine washable yarn as this generally keeps its shape and colour well. Bear in mind that because toys are usually well loved, they get dirty very quickly and may need frequent washing. Acrylic yarns are recommended because they are reasonably priced, machine washable, keep their colour well and come in a large range of attractive shades.

If you are going to make several toys, the larger balls of yarn generally work out cheaper. Always check your tension when starting a toy and should you use more than one brand of yarn, check the tension on the new brand.

When buying more than one ball of the same colour yarn, ensure that the dye lot number is the same, as even a minor difference in shade can be quite noticeable.

AMOUNT OF YARN

The main part of each toy can be made from 100 g of yarn or less and oddments can be used for the other parts. Many of the smaller toys can be made completely from leftover yarns.

Yarn amounts specified in the patterns can never be absolutely exact. This is partly due to the fact that tensions vary according to the knitter, but mostly because the number of metres (yards) per gram (ounce) varies. To ensure that you will not run out of yarn, the yarn amounts given in the instructions are generous.

EQUIPMENT

Pins: Always use glass/plastic-headed pins or knitter's pins, as ordinary pins could easily get lost in the knitting (or the stuffing), making the toy extremely dangerous.

Sewing needle: Use a yarn (knitter's) sewing needle for joining knitted pieces. It has a blunt point and will not split the yarn.

Stitch holders: These prevent stitches from unravelling when they are not in use. Alternatively, a spare knitting needle (ideally double pointed) can be used as a stitch holder. For holding just a few stitches a safety pin is useful.

Knitting needles: Available in seventeen different sizes, knitting needles range in size from 2 mm (old size 14) to 10 mm (old size 000). Specialist suppliers may have needles a couple of sizes larger and smaller than these, but they are rarely used. The table on page 8 will show you the old British and current American equivalents to metric sizes. Needle sizes are approximate and different makes will vary slightly.

TENSION

It is important to check your tension before you start knitting. Knit a swatch using the specified yarn and knitting needles. If there are too many stitches to 10 cm (4 in), your tension is tight and you should change to a larger sized needle. If there are too few stitches, your tension is loose and you should change to a smaller sized needle.

Opposite: Benge and Betsey Bunny (page 68), Jack (page 102), Baby Panda and Panda (page 60), Girl Octopus (page 124)

Right: *When oversewing seams together, insert the needle from back to front under the loops between the 'knots' at the edges of the knitting*

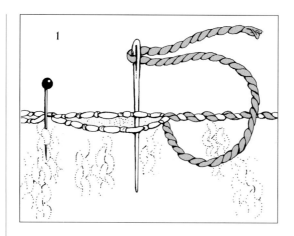

CASTING ON

Although there are many techniques for casting on stitches, the following cast-on method creates a firm and attractive edge:

First make a slip loop in the yarn and place the loop on the left-hand needle. Insert the point of the right-hand needle into the loop on the left-hand needle, wind the yarn round the right-hand needle and draw the yarn through the loop. Pass the new loop onto the left-hand needle and pull the yarn to tighten the new loop.

Next insert the right-hand needle between the two loops on the left-hand needle, wind the yarn round the right-hand needle and draw the yarn through. Slip the new loop onto the left-hand needle as before.

Continue in this way, inserting the needle between two loops on the left-hand needle, until you have the required number of stitches.

CASTING ON OR OFF LOOSELY

In some patterns you will be asked to cast off or cast on *loosely*. To cast on loosely use knitting needles two sizes larger than those called for in the pattern. In other words, if the pattern calls for 3¼ mm (old size 10) needles, use 4 mm (old size 8) knitting needles to cast on. Then change to 3¼ mm (old size 10) needles and continue following the instructions.

Cast off loosely by again changing to needles two sizes larger than those stated in the pattern.

BASIC STITCHES

Here is how to work the simple stitches used for the toys:

Stocking stitch: Alternate one row knit and one row purl. The knit side is the right side of the work.

Garter stitch: Knit every row. Both sides of the work are identical.

Reverse stocking stitch: Alternate one row knit and one row purl. The purl side is the right side of the work.

K1, P1 rib: Alternate one knit stitch with one purl stitch to the end of the row. On the next row, knit all the knit stitches and purl all the purl stitches as they face you.

Moss stitch: Alternate one knit stitch with one purl stitch to the end of the row. On the next row, knit all the purl stitches and purl all the knit stitches as they face you. Repeat the last row until the required number of rows have been worked.

JOINING YARN

Always join yarn (whether it be a new ball of yarn or a different colour) at the end of a row and never knot yarn as the knot may come through to the right side and spoil your work. Any long loose ends will be useful for sewing up afterwards.

SEAMS

There is no need to press the knitted pieces of the toys prior to sewing up.

Unless otherwise stated, oversew seams together (join row ends) with the right sides of the pieces

NEEDLE SIZES

British metric	2mm	2¼mm	2¾mm	3mm	3¼mm	3¾mm	4mm	4½mm	5mm	5½mm	6mm	6½mm	7mm	7½mm
American	0	1	2		3	5	6	7	8	9	10	10½		
British old sizes	14	13	12	11	10	9	8	7	6	5	4	3	2	1

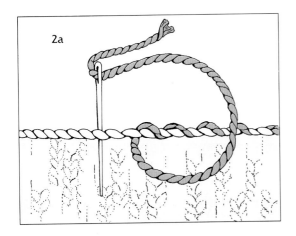

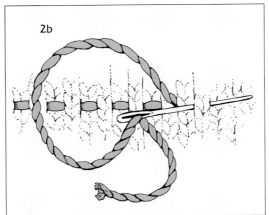

Far left: *To gather a cast-
on edge insert the
needle from back to
front under every other
loop along the edge,
then pull to gather*
Left: *One method for
gathering the doll's
neck is to work a run-
ning stitch along the
neck, then pull to gather*

together and the wrong sides facing outwards. Small pieces which are difficult to turn right side out are usually joined with the wrong sides facing each other.

When oversewing seams together, insert the needle from the back to the front under the loops between the 'knots' at the edges of the knitting (see Fig. 1).

FINISHING

The finishing instructions are featured at the end of each pattern. Read all the instructions carefully before sewing the toy together.

In general, it is best to knit up all the pieces before assembling the toy. Where there are numerous parts, however, it might be easier to make them up as you go along so you are not left with a confusing heap of pieces at the end.

Studying the picture of the toy will be your best guide to the finishing touches.

STUFFING

There are many different kinds of stuffing on the market. For knitted toys it is worth buying good quality. Always ensure that the stuffing is washable and that it meets the toy safety standard.

When making up, stuff the toys evenly so that they do not look lumpy. Make sure you stuff the toys firmly, unless otherwise stated, but do not overstuff. Tweezers are useful for stuffing thin or tiny pieces.

GATHERING

When finishing the toys you will need to know how to work these two simple gathering techniques.
Cast-on edge: To gather a cast-on edge, begin

by inserting the needle from back to front under every other loop along the cast-on edge. Then pull the yarn tightly to gather (see Fig. 2a).

Neck shaping: One way to shape the toy's neck after stuffing is simply to wrap a length of matching yarn once or twice around the neck, pull tightly, knot and sew ends into the back neck seam.

The neck can also be shaped by working a running stitch along it (see Fig. 2b). Work the running stitch over one knit stitch and under the next. When the stitching is complete pull the ends of the yarn tightly and knot.

For small toys (or other toys if desired) a combination of the two neck shaping methods can be used (see Fig. 2c). Leaving long loose ends at each end and beginning and ending at the back seam, work the running stitch over one half of each stitch and under the other half all around the neck. Pull both ends to gather and knot. Then wrap one end round the neck and knot at the back again.

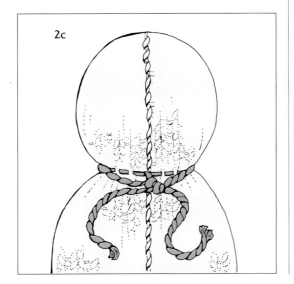

Left: *When gathering
the neck of a toy, leave
long loose ends to sew
into the back of the
neck at the seamline*

Right, top: *Double knitting yarn is made up of three or four single strands or 'plys'*
Right, bottom: *Stranded embroidery cotton is made up of six separate strands*

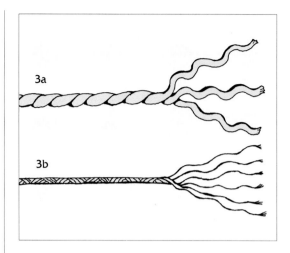

EMBROIDERY YARNS

Either knitting yarn (see Fig. 3a) or stranded embroidery cotton (see Fig. 3b) may be used for embroidering the toys.

Stranded embroidery cotton is made up of six strands which are easily separated. Generally, three strands are used for embroidering features on the toys' faces.

Ordinary knitting yarn is made up of two or more 'plys', or single strands, which have been twisted together. If you are using double knitting yarn for embroidering a mouth and nose on a toy, carefully separate out a single 'ply' of the yarn. This single strand makes delicate and effective facial features.

WORKING FACIAL FEATURES

Correct positioning of the eyes, nose and mouth is important for the overall appeal of the toy. Generally, you will find that the eyes are worked about halfway down the head.

Study the picture of the toy and try to copy the position of the features. It is sometimes best to work the features before sewing on the hair. For best results, mark the positions of the eyes, nose and mouth with glass-headed pins before starting your embroidery (see Fig. 5a).

EMBROIDERING EYES

Knotted eyes are especially attractive and are used on all the toys. The knot is worked onto a length of black yarn and then sewn firmly in place on the head.

To start with, cut a 30 cm (12 in) length of black yarn. Wind one end around the other as if

Far right: *To make a knotted eye, wind one end of the yarn round the other at least three times, then pull both ends to form an attractive oval shape*

beginning to knot the centre of the strand, but do not pull yet. Then wind one end round the other twice more as shown (see Fig. 4a). Wind the yarn around six times for larger toys and three times for smaller toys. Pull both ends of the yarn to form the knot (see Fig. 4b). This will create an attractive oval shape for the eye.

To make even bigger eyes for the very large toys (such as Alice and Andrew on page 16), use two strands of black yarn and wind the yarn six times through the knot.

Using a blunt-ended needle, sew each end separately in place on the toy's face so that the knotted eye is positioned vertically (see Fig. 5b). In order to hide the ends of the yarn, insert the needle at the eye position and bring it out at the top of the head. Fasten the ends securely to the head and trim them as short as possible. The hair will cover the trimmed ends.

On toys such as Ted and Teresa Bear (see page 56) or Betsey and Benge Bunny (see page 68), the ends can be fastened at the position of the arms so that the arms cover the fastened ends.

EMBROIDERING NOSES AND MOUTHS

Nose: The noses on most of the toys are worked by embroidering a simple horizontal straight stitch and working over the same stitches once or twice (see Fig. 5c).

As stated in the instructions for most of the toys, use a single 'ply' of double knitting yarn for the nose. Only the very large toys require a thicker thread.

Mouth: For a V-shaped mouth, work two straight stitches in the position marked by the pins (see Fig. 5d).

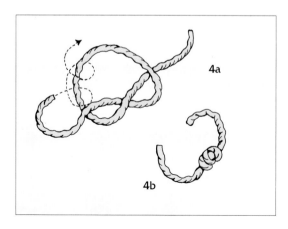

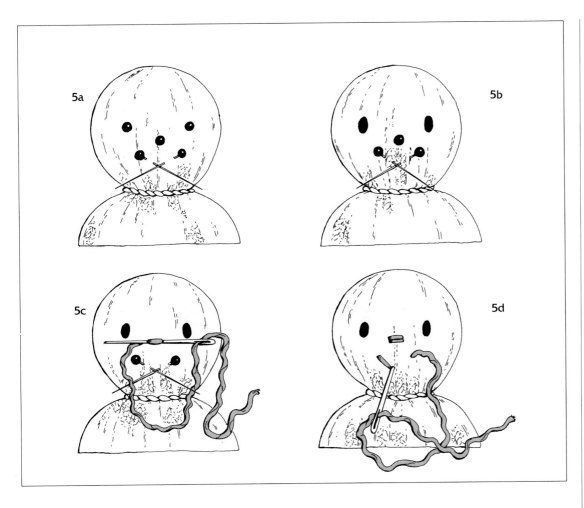

Left: *Working the facial features (diagrams show eye, nose and mouth positions marked with pins; completed knotted eyes; working the nose; working a V-shaped mouth)*

The semi-circular backstitch mouth is required for some of the medium-sized and most of the large-sized toys. It is worked from right to left and can be rounded off by weaving the yarn back to the beginning of the mouth, over and under each stitch (see Fig. 6).

TO COLOUR CHEEKS

The final finishing touch to most of the toys is colouring the cheeks. To do this, take a red colouring pencil, and stroke the knitting several times in a circular motion until the required cheek colour is achieved.

Note: Do not use a paint pencil as the colour will run when the toy is washed.

POMPONS

The finishing instructions for the toys sometimes call for a pompon. Pompons are quick and easy to make. Here are some helpful tips for making them full and fluffy.

To make a pompon, first cut out two circles of cardboard. The diameter of the cardboard should be the same as the required pompon size. Cut out centres that are approximately one third of the total diameter (see Fig. 7a).

Place the cardboard circles together and pass the yarn through the centre hole, over the outside edge, then through the centre again (see Fig. 7b).

Continue wrapping the yarn until the centre hole is full (see Fig. 7c).

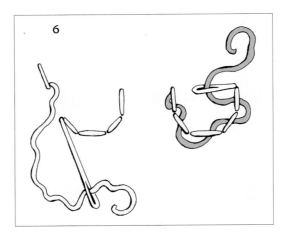

Left: *To round off a backstitch mouth, weave in and out under the finished stitches*

Right: *To make a pompon, cut two circles of cardboard, place them together, wrap yarn around until centre hole is full, then cut yarn all round edge of circle*

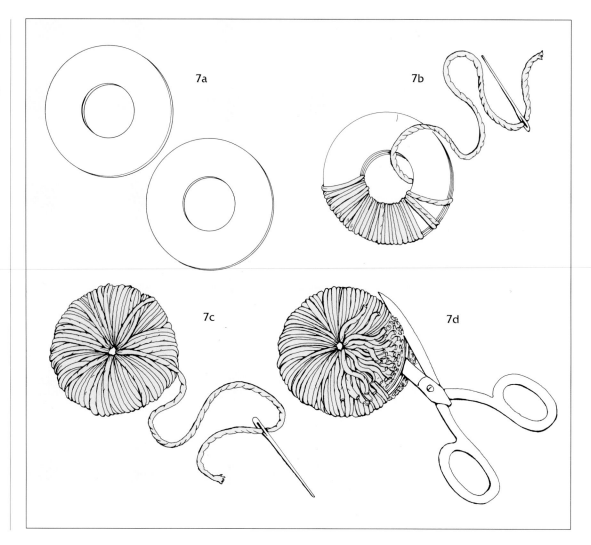

Below: *For long hair, tie bunched loops of yarn at one end, cut along fold at other end, then stitch to forehead to form a fringe; cover back of head with long strands of yarn and secure with backstitch along centre parting; attach plaits to side of face with a few stitches*

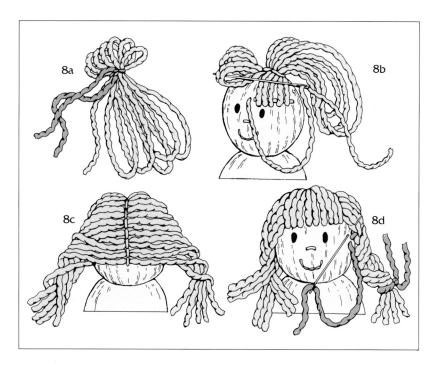

Cut through the yarn all around the edge of the circle (see Fig. 7d).

Then wrap a separate length of yarn around the centre, slipping it between the cardboard circles. Pull tightly and tie securely. The ends of this length of yarn are used to secure the pompon, so leave long loose ends. Carefully remove the cardboard.

Trim the pompon to the required size, but leave long loose ends to sew the pompon in place.

HAIR INSTRUCTIONS

Throughout the book you will find a variety of hair styles, all of which are very simple to work if you adhere to the following basic rules.

The hair is usually begun by wrapping yarn around a piece of card. It is best to use thick card for this because thin card will bend and you will end up with an uneven selection of loops/strands, thus making the hair more difficult to work and resulting in an uneven finish.

Slip the resulting bunch of loops off the card, then tie one end with a length of matching yarn and cut the other end along the fold (see Fig. 8a).

Always secure the fringe, bunches and plaits firmly to the head with a few stitches (see Fig. 8b, 8c, and 8d).

If you find that the hair looks too bulky, use a finer yarn or cut down on the number of strands used. Likewise, if the style looks a little sparse, just add a few more strands.

TWISTED CORDS

If a twisted cord is required when finishing a toy, make it as follows:

Take a length of yarn four times the length of the desired finished twisted cord. Fold the yarn in half and tie the two ends together. Hook the folded end around a door handle and turn the other end until the strands are tightly twisted. Keeping the cord tightly extended to avoid tangles, fold it in half and pinch the two ends together. Then allow the two halves to twist together around each other. Knot the two ends together and even out the twists.

BRITISH AND AMERICAN TERMINOLOGY

U.K.	U.S.A.
cast off	bind off
double knitting yarn*	heavy sport-weight yarn
dungarees	overalls
fringe (hair)	bangs
four-ply yarn	light sport-weight yarn
grams (g)	28 g = 1 oz
moss stitch	seed stitch
oversew	overcast
plaits	braids
slip loop	slip knot
spectacles	glasses
stocking stitch	stockinette stitch
tension	gauge
yarn forward (yfwd)	yarn over (yo)

*Sometimes labelled 'DK' or 'Quick Knit'.

ABBREVIATIONS

approx	approximately
cm	centimetre(s)
dec	decreas(e)(ing)
foll	follow(s)(ing)
g	gram(s)
in	inch(es)
inc	increas(e)(ing)
K	knit
LH	left hand
m	metre(s)
mm	millimetre(s)
P	purl
oz	ounce(s)
patt	pattern
rem	remain(s)(ing)
rep	repeat(s)(ing)
rev st st	reverse stocking stitch
RH	right hand
RS	right side(s)
st(s)	stitch(es)
st st	stocking stitch
tbl	through back of loop(s)
tog	together
WS	wrong side(s)
yd	yard(s)
yfwd	yarn forward (and over RH needle to form new loop)
( )	repeat instructions inside parentheses
*	repeat instructions between, from or before asterisks as instructed

DOLLY MIXTURES

ALICE AND ANDREW

It's back to school for Alice and Andrew, a delightful twosome in their smart school uniforms. They also have a colourful, mix 'n' match wardrobe of indoor and outdoor clothes to change into when classes are over.

MATERIALS FOR ALICE AND ANDREW

- Double knitting yarn: 100 g pink for each doll, 100 g light brown for hair for each doll
- Small amounts of double knitting yarn in red for nose and mouth, black for eyes and yellow for Alice's hair ribbons
- Pair of 3¼ mm (old size 10) knitting needles *or size to obtain correct tension*
- 260 g (9 oz) good quality washable stuffing for each doll
- Red pencil for cheeks

BASIC DOLL

SIZE Alice and Andrew each measure approx 44.5 cm (17½ in) in height, when worked in recommended tension

TENSION 27 sts and 38 rows to 10 cm (4 in) measured over st st and worked on 3¼ mm needles
Check your tension before beginning and change needle size if necessary.

BODY AND HEAD

The Alice and Andrew dolls are worked in exactly the same way except for their hair and Andrew's ears.
With pink, cast on 56 sts.
Starting with a K row, work 48 rows in st st, so ending with a P row.
This completes body.

NECK SHAPING
Next row (RS) (K2tog) 28 times. (28 sts)
P one row.
Next row K into front and back of each st. (56 sts)
Starting with a P row, work 43 rows more in st st for head, so ending with a P row.
Next row (RS) (K2tog) 28 times. (28 sts)
Next row (P2tog) 14 times. (14 sts)
Break off yarn leaving a long loose end.
Using a blunt-ended needle, thread loose end through all 14 sts on needle, pull yarn to gather tightly, then fasten off.

ARMS (make 2)

With pink, cast on 6 sts.
Start at top of arm as follows:
1st row (RS) K into front and back of first st, K to last st, K into front and back of last st.
2nd row P into front and back of first st, P to last st, P into front and back of last st.

Rep last 2 rows 4 times more. (26 sts)
Starting with a K row, work 20 rows in st st, so ending with a P row.

WRIST SHAPING
Next row (RS) K2tog, K to last 2 sts, K2tog. (24 sts)
Starting with a P row, work 3 rows in st st, so ending with a P row.

HAND SHAPING
***Next row** (RS) K into front and back of first st, K to last st, K into front and back of last st.
Starting with a P row, work 3 rows in st st, so ending with a P row.*
Rep from * to * once more. (28 sts)
Next row (RS) K2tog, K to last 2 sts, K2tog. (26 sts)
P one row.
Next row Cast off 3 sts, K to end. (23 sts)
Next row Cast off 3 sts, P to end. (20 sts)
Starting with a K row, work 4 rows in st st, so ending with a P row.
Next row (RS) (K2tog) 10 times. (10 sts)
P one row.
Cast off.

LEGS (make 2)

With pink, cast on 24 sts.
Start at bottom of foot as follows:
1st row (RS) K into front and back of each st. (48 sts)
Starting with a P row, work 13 rows in st st, so ending with a P row.

ANKLE SHAPING
Next row (RS) K6, (K2tog) twice, (K3tog) 9 times, (K2tog) twice, K7. (26 sts)
Starting with a P row, work 51 rows in st st for leg.
Cast off.

ANDREW'S EARS (make 2)

With pink, cast on 10 sts.

Starting with a K row, work 4 rows in st st, so ending with a P row.
Next row (RS) (K2tog) 5 times. (5 sts)
P one row.
Next row K into front and back of each st. (10 sts)
Starting with a P row, work 4 rows in st st, so ending with a K row.
Cast off purlwise.

ALICE'S RIBBONS (make 2)
With yellow, cast on 100 sts.
Cast off.

FINISHING

Body and head Join centre back seam (row ends) of body and head, leaving cast-on edge of body open. Turn right side out.

Stuff body and head firmly, then oversew cast-on edge of body tog, keeping seam at centre back.

To shape neck, using a long length of pink yarn, start at centre back neck and work running st along inc row of head. Pull both ends tightly to gather neck and knot at centre back. Then wrap one end of yarn once round neck, pull, knot at centre back and sew ends into neck.

Below: Detail of Alice and Andrew, showing hair and facial features

Arms Join bottom of hand and row ends of each arm up to top shaping. Turn arms right side out.

Stuff each arm firmly and sew cast-on edge and shaped edges of one arm to each side of body, with seams facing body and cast-on edges about 1 cm (¼ in) from neck.

Legs Join bottom of foot and centre back seam (row ends) of each leg, leaving cast-off edge of each leg open. Turn legs right side out.

Stuff each leg firmly and oversew top edge tog, keeping seam at centre back. Sew legs to lower edge of body.

Embroidery Using a single 'ply' of red yarn and working in backstitch, work semi-circle for mouth, then weave yarn in and out of back-stitches back to beginning and fasten off.

Using a single 'ply' of red yarn, work a short horizontal straight st and work twice over same st for nose.

Using black yarn, embroider eyes (see instructions on page 10).

Colour cheeks with red pencil.

Andrew's ears With wrong sides tog, join cast-on and cast-off edges tog, then join row ends. (Do not stuff.) Sew cast-on/cast-off edge of one ear to each side of head half way between top of head and neck.

Alice's hair Loosely wrap light brown yarn about 45 times round a 33 cm (13 in) piece of card. Slip looped yarn carefully off card, keeping it folded in half. Wrap a separate length of light brown yarn round strands 5 cm (2 in) from one folded end, pull tightly and knot. Cut the strands along the fold at the other end. Sew the tied section to top of head so that the folded loops fall over forehead to form a fringe and the cut ends hang down over back of head. Spread fringe out and sew in place (see page 12).

Wrap light brown yarn about 210 times round a 27 cm (10½ in) piece of card. (If this becomes too bulky cut lengths in a few smaller bunches.) Cut strands along one end of card. Keeping cut ends coming from fringe swept toward back of head, lay the new strands carefully over back of head so that they cover head from tied section of fringe to back neck and so that the centre of the strands lie along a centre parting. To secure the strands in place work backstitch from tied section of fringe to centre back neck (this also forms a centre hair parting).

Plait hair, using about 85 strands for each of three sections of plait. Tie a length of yarn at end of each plait to secure. Work a few stitches along sides of face to secure hair in place. Tie knitted ribbons into bows at ends of plaits then trim ends of plaits.

Andrew's hair Loosely wrap light brown yarn about 14 times round a 3 cm (1¼ in) piece of card. Slip the looped yarn carefully off the card,

making sure that it remains folded in half. Wrap a separate length of light brown yarn round the centre of the looped yarn, then pull tightly and knot. This forms one bunch of curls. Make enough bunched curls in the same way to cover the head with hair and stitch the curls closely tog in place.

✿ ✿

MATERIALS FOR PANTS

- 4-ply knitting yarn: 20 g white each for Andrew's and Alice's pants
- Pair each of 2¾ mm (old size 12) and 3¼ mm (old size 10) knitting needles *or size to obtain correct tension*
- 30 cm (12 in) of 5 mm (¼ in) wide elastic for each pair of pants

MATERIALS FOR T-SHIRT

- Double knitting yarn: 40 g white for each T-shirt
- Pair each of 3¼ mm (old size 10) and 4 mm (old size 8) knitting needles *or size to obtain correct tension*
- Three 11 mm (⅜ in) white buttons

ALICE'S AND ANDREW'S CLOTHES

TENSIONS 27 sts and 38 rows to 10 cm (4 in) measured over st st and worked on 3¼ mm needles, using double knitting yarn

23 sts and 32 rows to 10 cm (4 in) measured over st st and worked on 3¼ mm needles, using 2 strands of double knitting yarn

23 sts and 34 rows to 10 cm (4 in) measured over st st and worked on 4 mm needles, using double knitting yarn

32 sts and 40 rows to 10 cm (4 in) measured over st st and worked on 3¼ mm needles, using 4-ply knitting yarn

Check your tension before beginning and change needle size if necessary.

PANTS

TO MAKE
The 2 legs are worked separately and then joined at the top.

FIRST LEG
**With 3¼ mm needles and white, cast on 42 sts.

Starting with a K row, work 4 rows in st st, so ending with a P row.

Work hemline fold on *Alice's pants only* on next row as follows:

Next row (picot row) (RS) *Yfwd, K2tog, rep from * to end. (42 sts)

Work hemline fold on *Andrew's pants only* on next row as follows:

Next row (RS) Purl.

Continue leg on *both Alice's and Andrew's pants* as follows:

Starting with a P row, work 5 rows in st st, so ending with a P row.**

Break off yarn and slip sts onto a spare needle.

SECOND LEG
Rep from ** to ** for second leg. Do not break off yarn.

JOINING LEGS
With RS facing, P42 sts of second leg, then P42 sts of first leg from spare needle. (84 sts)

Starting with a P row, work 17 rows in st st, so ending with a P row.

WAISTBAND
Change to 2¾ mm needles.

Next row (RS) *K1, P1, rep from * to end.

Rep last row 4 times more.

K one row (WS) for foldline.

Starting with a K row, work 5 rows in st st for waistband facing, so ending with a K row.

Cast off purlwise.

FINISHING
Join centre back seam (row ends) of pants from cast-off edge to point where legs were joined on, then join each leg seam (row ends) separately.

Fold hem of pant legs to WS (along picot row *for Alice's pants* and along first P row *for Andrew's pants*) and sew in place.

Fold waistband facing to WS along foldline and sew in place, leaving a small opening. Insert elastic through opening and thread through waistband. Trim elastic to fit doll snugly, sew ends tog and sew up opening.

T-SHIRT

SLEEVES (make 2)
With 4 mm needles, cast on 37 sts.

K 4 rows (garter st).

P one row.

RAGLAN SHAPING
***Next row** (RS) Cast off 3 sts, K to end. (34 sts)

MATERIALS FOR SCHOOL CARDIGAN

· Double knitting yarn: 70 g blue for each cardigan
· Pair each of 3¼ mm (old size 10) and 4 mm (old size 8) knitting needles *or size to obtain correct tension*
· Five 11 mm (⅜ in) blue buttons

Next row Cast off 3 sts, P to end. (31 sts)
*Next row** K2, K2tog, K to last 4 sts, K2tog tbl, K2.
P one row.*
Rep from * to * 7 times more. (15 sts)
Break off yarn and slip sts onto a st holder.***

BACK

With 4 mm needles, cast on 37 sts.
K 4 rows (garter st).
Starting with a P row, work 15 rows in st st, so ending with a P row.**

RAGLAN ARMHOLE SHAPING

Complete as for sleeves from *** to ***.

FRONT

Work as for back to **.

DIVIDE FOR NECK OPENING

Next row (RS) Cast off 3 sts, K12 (13 sts now on RH needle), turn leaving rem 21 sts on a st holder.
Working on these 13 sts of first side of neck only, continue as follows:
P one row.
*Next row** K2, K2tog, K to end.
P one row.*
Rep from * to * 6 times more. (6 sts)
Next row K2, (K2tog) twice. (4 sts)
Next row P2tog, P2. (3 sts)
Break off yarn and slip these sts onto a st holder.
Return to 21 sts on first st holder and with RS facing, slip centre 5 sts onto a safety pin for buttonhole band, rejoin yarn to rem sts and K to end. (16 sts)
Next row (WS) Cast off 3 sts, P to end. (13 sts)
*Next row** K to last 4 sts, K2tog tbl, K2.
P one row.*
Rep from * to * 6 times more. (6 sts)
Next row K2tog, K2tog tbl, K2. (4 sts)
Next row P2, P2tog. (3 sts)
Do not break off yarn.

COLLAR

With 3¼ mm needles and with RS facing, K3 sts of right front, K15 sts of one sleeve from st holder, K15 sts of back from st holder, K15 sts of 2nd sleeve from st holder and K3 sts of left front from st holder. (51 sts)
Next row (WS) *K1, P1, rep from * to last st, K1.
Next row *P1, K1, rep from * to last st, P1.

Rep last 2 rows 5 times more.
Cast off loosely in rib.

FRONT BUTTONHOLE BAND

With 3¼ mm needles and with RS facing, work across 5 sts at centre front on safety pin as follows:
Work 4 rows in K1, P1 rib as for collar.
Keeping K1, P1 rib correct as set throughout, work first buttonhole on next row as follows:
Buttonhole row *Rib 2, yfwd, work next 2 sts tog, rib 1.
**Work 7 rows in rib.
Rep buttonhole row once more.**
Rep from ** to ** once more.
Work 2 rows in rib.
Cast off in rib.

FRONT BUTTON BAND

With 3¼ mm needles, cast on 5 sts.
Work 23 rows in K1, P1 rib as for collar.
Cast off in rib.

FINISHING

Join raglan sleeve seams, then join side and sleeve seams.
  Sew side of buttonhole band to right side of front opening *for Alice's T-shirt* and to left side of front opening *for Andrew's T-shirt*. Sew side of button band to other side of front opening, then sew bottom edge of button band to WS of centre front behind buttonhole band.
  Sew three buttons to button band to correspond with buttonholes.

SCHOOL CARDIGAN

SLEEVES (make 2)

With 3¼ mm needles, cast on 37 sts.
1st rib row (RS) *K1, P1, rep from * to last st, K1.
2nd rib row *P1, K1, rep from * to last st, P1.
Rep last 2 rows twice more.
Change to 4 mm needles.
Starting with a K row, work 16 rows in st st, so ending with a P row.

RAGLAN SHAPING

Complete as for T-shirt sleeve from *** to ***.

BACK

With 3¼ mm needles, cast on 41 sts.
Work 6 rows in K1, P1 rib as for sleeve.

Change to 4 mm needles.

Starting with a K row, work 16 rows in st st, so ending with a P row.

RAGLAN ARMHOLE SHAPING

***Next row** (RS) Cast off 3 sts, K to end. (38 sts)

Next row Cast off 3 sts, P to end. (35 sts)

*Next row** K2, K2tog, K to last 4 sts, K2tog tbl, K2.

P one row.*

Rep from * to * 7 times more. (19 sts)

Break off yarn and slip sts onto a st holder.***

LEFT FRONT

With 3¼ mm needles, cast on 23 sts.

Work 4 rows in K1, P1 rib as for sleeve.

For Alice's cardigan rib one row more, but *for Andrew's cardigan*, keeping rib correct as set, work buttonhole on 5th rib row as follows:

Buttonhole row (RS) Rib to last 3 sts, yfwd, work next 2 sts tog, rib 1.

For both Andrew's and Alice's cardigan work one row more in rib (6 rib rows in all from cast-on edge).

Change to 4 mm needles.

Next row (RS) K18, then slip rem 5 sts onto a safety pin for front band.

Starting with a P row, work 15 rows in st st, so ending with a P row.

RAGLAN ARMHOLE SHAPING

***Next row** (RS) Cast off 3 sts, K to end. (15 sts)

P one row.

*Next row** K2, K2tog, K to end.

P one row.*

Rep from * to * 5 times more. (9 sts)

Next row (RS) K2, K2tog, K to last 2 sts, K2tog.

Next row P2tog, P to end.**

Rep from ** to ** once more. (3 sts)

Break off yarn and slip sts onto a st holder.***

ALICE'S FRONT BAND

With 3¼ mm needles and RS facing, rejoin yarn to 5 sts on safety pin and work 30 rows in rib, so ending with a WS row.

Break off yarn and slip sts onto safety pin for neckband.

ANDREW'S FRONT BAND

With 3¼ mm needles and RS facing, rejoin yarn to 5 sts on safety pin and work 6 rows in rib, so ending with a WS row.

****Buttonhole row** (RS) Rib 2, yfwd, work 2 sts tog, rib 1.

Rib 7 rows.****

Andrew wearing school uniform

MATERIALS FOR PLEATED SKIRT

- Double knitting yarn: 50 g grey
- Pair each of 3¼ mm (old size 10) and 4 mm (old size 8) knitting needles *or size to obtain correct tension*
- 30 cm (12 in) of 5 mm (¼ in) wide elastic

MATERIALS FOR SHORTS

- Double knitting yarn: 40 g grey
- Pair each of 3¼ mm (old size 10) and 4 mm (old size 8) knitting needles *or size to obtain correct tension*
- 30 cm (12 in) of 5 mm (¼ in) wide elastic

MATERIALS FOR SOCKS

- 4-ply knitting yarn: 20 g white for each pair of socks
- Pair each of 2¾ mm (old size 12) and 3¼ mm (old size 10) knitting needles *or size to obtain correct tension*

Rep from **** to **** twice more.
Break off yarn and slip sts onto a safety pin for neckband.

RIGHT FRONT

With 3¼ mm needles, cast on 23 sts.
Work 4 rows in K1, P1 rib as for sleeve.
For Andrew's cardigan rib one row more, but *for Alice's cardigan*, keeping rib correct as set, work buttonhole on 5th rib row as follows:
Buttonhole row (RS) Rib 2, yfwd, work next 2 sts tog, rib to end.
For both Andrew's and Alice's cardigan work one row more in rib (6 rib rows in all from cast-on edge).
Next row (RS) Rib first 5 sts and slip these sts onto a safety pin for front band, change to 4 mm needles and K to end. (18 sts)
Starting with a P row, work 16 rows in st st, so ending with a K row.

RAGLAN ARMHOLE SHAPING

***Next row** (WS) Cast off 3 sts, P to end. (15 sts)
*Next row** K to last 4 sts, K2tog tbl, K2. P one row.*
Rep from * to * 5 times more. (9 sts)
Next row (RS) K2tog, K to last 4 sts, K2tog tbl, K2.
Next row P to last 2 sts, P2tog.**
Rep from ** to ** once more. (3 sts)
Break off yarn and slip sts onto a st holder.***

ANDREW'S FRONT BAND

With 3¼ mm needles and WS facing, rejoin yarn to 5 sts on safety pin and work 29 rows in rib, so ending with a WS row.
Do not break off yarn.

ALICE'S FRONT BAND

With 3¼ mm needles and WS facing, rejoin yarn to 5 sts on safety pin and work 5 rows in rib, so ending with a WS row.
****Buttonhole row** (RS) Rib 2, yfwd, work 2 sts tog, rib 1.
Rib 7 rows.****
Rep from **** to **** twice more.
Do not break off yarn.

NECKBAND

With 3¼ mm needles and with RS facing, rib 5 sts of right front band, pick up and K4 sts up neck shaping, K3 sts of right front from st holder, K15 sts of one sleeve from st holder, K19 sts of back from st holder, K15 sts of 2nd sleeve from st holder, K3 sts of left front from

st holder, pick up and K4 sts down neck shaping, rib 5 sts of left front band from safety pin. (73 sts)
For Alice's neckband work next row as follows:
Next row (WS) Rib to last 3 sts, yfwd, work next 2 sts tog, rib 1.
For Andrew's neckband work next row as follows:
Next row (WS) Rib 2, yfwd, work next 2 sts tog, rib to end.
Work 2 rows more in rib, ending with a WS row.
Next row (RS) *K1, K2tog, rep from * to last st, K1. (49 sts).
Cast off loosely knitwise.

FINISHING

Join raglan sleeve seams, then join side and sleeve seams.
  Sew front bands in place. Sew five buttons to button band to correspond with buttonholes.

PLEATED SKIRT

TO MAKE

With 4 mm needles and using grey yarn, cast on 120 sts.
1st row (WS) Knit.
2nd row (RS) *K6, P2, rep from * to end.
3rd row *K2, P6, rep from * to end.
Rep last 2 rows (2nd and 3rd rows) 15 times more, so ending with a WS row.

WAIST SHAPING

Next row (RS) *K2, K2tog, K2, P2tog, rep from * to end. (90 sts)
Next row *P2tog, P4, rep from * to end. (75 sts)

WAISTBAND

Change to 3¼ mm needles.
Next row (RS) *K1, P1, rep from * to last st, K1.
Next row *P1, K1, rep from * to last st, P1.
Rep last 2 rows once more.
P one row (RS) for foldline.
Starting with a P row, work 4 rows in st st for waistband facing.
Cast off loosely purlwise.

FINISHING

With right sides tog, join centre back skirt seam (row ends).
  Fold waistband facing to WS along foldline and sew in place, leaving a small opening. Insert elastic through opening and thread through waistband. Trim elastic to fit doll snugly, sew ends tog and sew up opening.

Alice wearing school uniform

SCHOOL SHORTS

TO MAKE

The 2 legs are worked separately and then joined at the top.

FIRST LEG

*With 4 mm needles and grey, cast on 40 sts.
K 4 rows (garter st).
Starting with a P row, work 3 rows in st st, so ending with a P row.*
Break off yarn and slip sts onto a spare needle.

SECOND LEG

Rep from * to * for second leg. Do not break off yarn.

JOINING LEGS

With RS facing, K40 sts of second leg, then K40 sts of first leg from spare needle. (80 sts)
Starting with a P row, work 15 rows in st st, so ending with a P row.

WAISTBAND

Change to 3¼ mm needles.
Next row (RS) *K1, P1, rep from * to end.
Rep last row 3 times more.
P one row (RS) for foldline.
Starting with a P row, work 4 rows in st st for waistband facing. Cast off loosely.

POCKET

With 4 mm needles and grey, cast on 12 sts.
Starting with a K row, work 10 rows in st st, so ending with a P row.
P one row. Cast off knitwise.

FINISHING

Join centre back seam (row ends) of shorts from the cast-off edge to the point where legs were joined on, then join each leg seam (row ends) separately.

Fold waistband facing to WS along foldline and sew in place, leaving a small opening. Insert elastic through opening and thread through waistband. Trim elastic to fit doll snugly, sew ends tog and sew up opening.

Sew pocket to one side of back of shorts with garter st edge at top.

SOCKS

TO MAKE

With 3¼ mm needles and white, cast on 32 sts.
1st row (RS) K into front and back of each st. (64 sts)

MATERIALS FOR SHOES

- Double knitting yarn: 20 g black (or brown) for each pair of shoes
- Pair of 3¼ mm (old size 10) knitting needles *or size to obtain correct tension*

MATERIALS FOR WILDLIFE JUMPER

- Double knitting yarn: 50 g light blue, 15 g green and a small amount of yellow and black for embroidery
- Black stranded cotton embroidery thread
- Pair each of 3¼ mm (old size 10) and 4 mm (old size 8) knitting needles *or size to obtain correct tension*
- Three 11 mm (⅜ in) light blue buttons
- Yellow and white felt

Cut one from yellow felt

Cut two from white felt

Starting with a P row, work 17 rows in st st, so ending with a P row.

Next row (RS) K14, (K2tog) twice, (K3tog) 9 times, (K2tog) twice, K15. (42 sts)

Starting with a P row, work 11 rows in st st *for short socks* or 25 rows in st st *for long socks*, so ending with a P row.

Change to 2¾ mm needles.

Next row (RS) *K1, P1, rep from * to end.

Rep last row 4 times more.

Cast off loosely in rib.

Make 2nd sock in same way.

FINISHING

Fold sock in half with RS tog and join row ends, then join bottom of sock.

SHOES

TO MAKE

With black (or brown), cast on 32 sts.

1st row (RS) K into front and back of each st. (64 sts)

Starting with a P row, work 13 rows in st st, so ending with a P row.

Next row (RS) K14, (K2tog) twice, (K3tog) 9 times, (K2tog) twice, K15. (42 sts)

K 3 rows (garter st).

Cast off loosely.

Make 2nd shoe in same way.

FINISHING

Fold shoe in half with right sides tog and join row ends, then join bottom of shoe.

For straps for Alice's shoes only, make a 46 cm (18 in) twisted cord (see instructions given on page 13) for each shoe. Sew centre of each cord to top of centre back seam of shoe. Tie ends in bow at front of leg.

WILDLIFE JUMPER

SLEEVES (make 2)

With 3¼ mm needles and light blue, cast on 36 sts.

1st rib row *K1, P1, rep from * to end.

Rep last row 5 times more.

Change to 4 mm needles.

Starting with a K row, work 20 rows in st st.

Cast off loosely.

BACK

With 3¼ mm needles and light blue, cast on 37 sts.

1st rib row (RS) *K1, P1, rep from * to last st, K1.

2nd rib row *P1, K1, rep from * to last st, P1.

Rep last 2 rows twice more.**

Change to 4 mm needles.

Starting with a K row, work 20 rows in st st, so ending with a P row.

DIVIDE FOR NECK OPENING

Next row (RS) K16, turn leaving rem 21 sts on a st holder.

Working on these 16 sts of first side of neck only, continue as follows:

Starting with a P row, work 17 rows in st st, so ending with a P row.

Next row (RS) Cast off first 10 sts, K to end. (6 sts)

Break off yarn and slip these sts onto a st holder.

Return to 21 sts on first st holder and with RS facing, slip centre 5 sts onto a safety pin for buttonhole band, rejoin yarn to rem sts and K to end. (16 sts)

Starting with a P row, work 17 rows in st st, so ending with a P row.

Next row (RS) K to last 10 sts, cast off last 10 st. (6 sts)

Break off yarn and slip these sts onto a st holder.

FRONT

Work as for back to **.

Change to 4 mm needles.

Starting with a K row, work 14 rows in st st in green and light blue, following 14 chart rows for colours, so ending with a P row.

Break off green yarn and complete with light blue only.

Starting with a K row, work 20 rows more in st st, so ending with a P row.

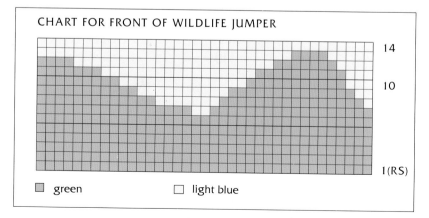

CHART FOR FRONT OF WILDLIFE JUMPER

14

10

1 (RS)

◼ green   ☐ light blue

NECK SHAPING

Next row (RS) K14, turn leaving rem 23 sts on a st holder.

Working on these 14 sts of first side of neck only, continue as follows:

Next row P2tog, P12.

Next row K11, K2tog.

Next row P2tog, P10.

K one row.

Next row P2tog, P9. (10 sts)

Starting with a K row, work 3 rows in st st, so ending with a K row.

Cast off purlwise.

Return to 23 sts on first st holder and with RS facing, slip centre 9 sts onto a st holder for neckband, rejoin yarn to rem sts and K to end. (14 sts)

Next row P12, P2tog.

Next row K2tog, K11.

Next row P10, P2tog.

K one row.

Next row P9, P2tog. (10 sts)

Starting with a K row, work 3 rows in st st, so ending with a K row.

Cast off purlwise.

BACK BANDS

The button band is worked separately and sewn on. The buttonhole band is worked from the 5 sts at the centre back opening.

BUTTON BAND

With 3¼ mm needles and light blue, cast on 5 sts.

Work 18 rows in K1, P1 rib as for back.

Break off yarn and slip sts onto a safety pin.

BUTTONHOLE BAND

With 3¼ mm needles and light blue, and with RS facing, work across 5 sts at centre back on safety pin as follows:

Work 4 rows in K1, P1 rib as for back.

Keeping K1, P1 rib correct as set throughout, work first buttonhole on next row as follows:

Buttonhole row *Rib 2, yfwd, work next 2 sts tog, rib 1.

Work 7 rows in rib.

Rep buttonhole row once more.

Work 5 rows in rib, so ending with a WS row.

Do not break off yarn.

NECKBAND

With 3¼ mm needles and light blue, and with RS facing, rib 5 sts of buttonhole band, K6 sts of left back from st holder, pick up and K8 sts

Andrew wearing wildlife jumper and long trousers

Alice wearing T-shirt and pinafore

down left front neck, K9 sts of centre front from st holder, pick up and K8 sts up right front neck, K6 sts of right back from st holder and rib 5 sts of button band from safety pin. (47 sts)
Next row (WS) Rib 44 sts, yfwd, work next 2 sts tog, rib 1.
Rib 2 rows.
Cast off loosely in rib.

FINISHING

Join shoulder seams. Place the centre of the top of each sleeve at the shoulder seam and sew the top of each sleeve to the back and front. Join the side and sleeve seams.

Sew side of buttonhole band to back opening. Sew side of button band to other side of opening, then sew bottom edge of button band to WS of centre back behind buttonhole band.
Appliqué Cut two sheep from white felt, and cut circle of yellow felt for sun (see diagram on page 24). Using sewing thread, sew sheep and sun to front (see photograph).

Using black yarn, work straight sts for four legs on each sheep. Using yellow yarn, work straight sts, radiating out around sun. Using black embroidery cotton, embroider eyes and mouth on sheep and eyes, nose and mouth on sun.

Sew three buttons to button band to correspond with buttonholes.

LONG TROUSERS

TROUSER LEGS (make 2)

The trousers are worked in 2 separate pieces.
With 4 mm needles and blue, cast on 50 sts.
K 4 rows (garter st).
Starting with a P row, work 39 rows in st st, so ending with a P row.

CRUTCH SHAPING

***Next row** (RS) K2tog, K to last 2 sts, K2tog.
Next row P2tog, P to last 2 sts, P2tog.*
Rep from * to * once more. (42 sts)
Next row (RS) K2tog, K to last 2 sts, K2tog. (40 sts)
Starting with a P row, work 9 rows in st st, so ending with a P row.

WAISTBAND

Change to 3¼ mm needles.
Next row (RS) *K1, P1, rep from * to end.
Rep last row 3 times more.

P one row (RS) for foldline.
Starting with a P row, work 4 rows in st st for waistband facing.
Cast off loosely.
Make second piece in same way.

FINISHING

Join two pieces of trousers at centre back seam (row ends) from cast-off edge end of crutch shaping. Join centre front seam in same way. Then join each leg seam.

Fold waistband facing to WS along foldline and sew in place, leaving a small opening. Insert elastic through opening and thread through waistband. Trim elastic to fit doll snugly, sew ends tog and sew up opening.

PINAFORE

SKIRT

With 4 mm needles and red, cast on 120 sts.
K 4 rows (garter st).
Starting with a P row, work 27 rows in st st, so ending with a P row.

WAIST SHAPING
Next row (RS) *K1, K2tog, rep from * to end. (80 sts)
P one row.

WAISTBAND
Change to 3¼ mm needles.
Next row (RS) *K1, P1, rep from * to end.
Rep last row 3 times more.
P one row (RS) for foldline.
Starting with a P row, work 4 rows in st st for waistband facing.
Cast off loosely purlwise.

BIB

With 4 mm needles and red and with RS facing, pick up and K22 centre sts along P row (centre row of waistband which forms foldline) so that there are 29 sts unworked along waistband on either side of bib.
*Next row** (WS) K3, P16, K3.
K one row.*
Rep from * to * 7 times more.
K 4 rows (garter st).
Cast off knitwise.

BIB STRAPS (make 2)

With 3¼ mm needles and red, cast on 40 sts.
K 2 rows (garter st).

Next row (buttonhole row) K2, K2tog, yfwd, K to end. (40 sts)
K 2 rows.
Cast off.

FINISHING

Finish skirt and insert elastic as for pleated skirt. Sew end (without buttonhole) of one strap to each side of centre back seam at top of waistband. Sew one button to each top corner of bib.

ANDREW'S WINTER JACKET

POCKETS (make 2)

With single strand of yarn, cast on 12 sts.
Starting with a K row, work 8 rows in st st, so ending with a P row.
K 3 rows (garter st). Cast off knitwise.

SLEEVES (make 2)

Note: All pieces of the jacket, except for the pockets, are worked with yarn used double.
With yarn double, cast on 37 sts.
K 4 rows (garter st).
Starting with a P row, work 19 rows in st st, so ending with a P row.
RAGLAN SHAPING
Complete as for T-shirt sleeve from *** to ***.

BACK

With yarn double, cast on 41 sts.
K 4 rows (garter st).
Starting with a P row, work 19 rows in st st, so ending with a P row.
RAGLAN SHAPING
Complete as for school cardigan back from *** to ***.

LEFT FRONT

With yarn double, cast on 23 sts.
K 3 rows (garter st).
Next row (RS) K18, then slip rem 5 sts onto a safety pin for front band.
Starting with a P row, work 19 rows in st st, so ending with a P row.
RAGLAN SHAPING
Complete left front as for school cardigan left front from *** to ***.
FRONT BAND
With yarn double and RS facing, rejoin yarn to 5 sts on safety pin and K 46 rows (garter st), so ending with a WS row.

MATERIALS FOR LONG TROUSERS

· Double knitting yarn: 75 g blue
· Pair each of 3¼ mm (old size 10) and 4 mm (old size 8) knitting needles *or size to obtain correct tension*
· 30 cm (12 in) of 5 mm (¼ in) wide elastic

MATERIALS FOR PINAFORE

· Double knitting yarn: 70 g red
· Pair each of 3¼ mm (old size 10) and 4 mm (old size 8) knitting needles *or size to obtain correct tension*
· 30 cm (12 in) of 5 mm (¼ in) wide elastic
· Two 11 mm (⅜ in) red buttons

MATERIALS FOR WINTER JACKET

· Double knitting yarn: 100 g dark green
· Pair of 3¼ mm (old size 10) knitting needles *or size to obtain correct tension*
· Five small snap fasteners (size 0)

MATERIALS FOR DUFFLE COAT

- Double knitting yarn: 100 g red and small amount in beige for toggles
- Pair each of 3¼ mm (old size 10) and 4 mm (old size 8) knitting needles *or size to obtain correct tension*
- One 5mm (³⁄₁₆ in) diameter plastic drinking straw

Opposite: Alice wearing duffle coat, and Andrew wearing winter jacket and long trousers

Break off yarn and slip sts onto a safety pin for neckband.

RIGHT FRONT

With yarn double, cast on 23 sts.
K 3 rows (garter st).
Next row (RS) K first 5 sts and slip these sts onto a safety pin for front band, K to end. (18 sts)
Starting with a P row, work 20 rows in st st, so ending with a K row.

RAGLAN SHAPING
Complete right front as for school cardigan right front from *** to ***.

FRONT BAND
With yarn double and WS facing, rejoin yarn to 5 sts on safety pin and K 45 rows (garter st), so ending with a WS row.
Do not break off yarn.

COLLAR
With yarn double and with RS facing, K5 sts of right front band, pick up and K4 sts up neck shaping, K3 sts of right front from st holder, K15 sts of one sleeve from st holder, K19 sts of back from st holder, K15 sts of 2nd sleeve from st holder, K3 sts of left front from st holder, pick up and K4 sts down neck shaping, K5 sts from safety pin. (73 sts)
Next row (WS) K5, P63, K5.
K one row.
Next row K5, P63, K5.
Next row Cast off 5 sts, *K2tog, K1, rep from * to last 7 sts, K2tog, K5. (47 sts)
Next row Cast off 5 sts, K to end. (42 sts)
K 12 rows (garter st).
Cast off loosely.

FINISHING
Join raglan sleeve seams, then join side and sleeve seams.
  Sew front bands in place. Sew one pocket to each front 2.5 cm (1 in) up from cast-on edge.
  Sew 5 snap fasteners to front opening.

ALICE'S DUFFLE COAT

POCKETS (make 2)
With 4 mm needles and red, cast on 11 sts.
Starting at bottom of pocket and starting with a K row, work 12 rows in st st, so ending with a P row.
Change to 3¼ mm needles.

P one row (RS) for foldline.
Starting with a P row, work 4 rows in st st for hem. Cast off.

SLEEVES (make 2)
With 3¼ mm needles and red, cast on 46 sts.
Starting with a K row, work 4 rows in st st for hem, so ending with a P row.
P one row (RS) for foldline.
Change to 4 mm needles.
Starting with a P row, work 23 rows in st st, so ending with a P row.

RAGLAN SHAPING
*****Next row** (RS) Cast off 3 sts, K to end. (43 sts)
Next row Cast off 3 sts, P to end. (40 sts)
***Next row** K2, K2tog, K to last 4 sts, K2tog tbl, K2.
P one row.*
Rep from * to * 8 times more. (22 sts)
Break off yarn and slip sts onto a st holder.***

BACK
With 3¼ mm needles and red, cast on 46 sts.
Starting with a K row, work 4 rows in st st for hem, so ending with a P row.
P one row (RS) for foldline.
Change to 4 mm needles.
Starting with a P row, work 39 rows in st st, so ending with a P row.

RAGLAN SHAPING
Complete as for sleeve from *** to ***.

LEFT FRONT
With 3¼ mm needles and red, cast on 28 sts.
Starting with a K row, work 4 rows in st st for hem, so ending with a P row.
P one row (RS) for foldline.***
Change to 4 mm needles.
Cast on 4 sts at end of last row. (32 sts)
Starting with a P row, work 39 rows in st st, so ending with a P row.

RAGLAN SHAPING
Next row (RS) Cast off 3 sts, K to end. (29 sts)
*P one row.
Next row K2, K2tog, K to end.*
Rep from * to * 5 times more. (23 sts)
Next row (WS) Cast off 4 sts, K to last 10 sts, then turn leaving last 10 sts on a st holder.
Working on these 9 sts only, continue as follows:
Starting with a K row, work 4 rows in st st for neck edge facing.
Cast off these 9 sts.

MATERIALS FOR SCARF AND MITTENS

- Double knitting yarn: 40 g mid-blue or light blue
- Pair of 3¼ mm (old size 10) knitting needles *or size to obtain correct tension*
- 2.5 mm crochet hook for fringe

MATERIALS FOR POMPON HAT

- Double knitting yarn: 40 g mid-blue
- Pair each of 3¼ mm (old size 10) and 4 mm (old size 8) knitting needles *or size to obtain correct tension*

Return to 10 sts on st holder and with WS facing, rejoin yarn and P one row.
**Next row K2, K2tog, K to end.
P one row.**
Rep from ** to ** once more. (8 sts)
Break off yarn and slip sts onto a st holder.

RIGHT FRONT

Work as for left front to ***.
Change to 4 mm needles.
P one row.
Cast on 4 sts at end of last row. (32 sts)
Starting with a K row, work 39 rows in st st, so ending with a K row.
RAGLAN SHAPING
Next row (WS) Cast off 3 sts, P to end. (29 sts)
*Next row K to last 4 sts, K2tog tbl, K2.
P one row.*
Rep from * to * 5 times more. (23 sts)
Next row (RS) Cast off 4 sts, P to last 10 sts, then turn leaving last 10 sts on a st holder.
Working on these 9 sts only, continue as follows:
Starting with a P row, work 4 rows in st st for neck edge facing.
Cast off these 9 sts purlwise.
Return to 10 sts on st holder and with RS facing, rejoin yarn and K to last 4 sts, K2tog tbl, K2.
P one row.
Next row K to last 4 sts, K2tog tbl, K2. (8 sts)
P one row.
Do not slip sts off needle and do not break off yarn.

HOOD

With 4 mm needles and with RS facing, cast on 4 sts at end of last row of right front, then work as follows:
K4 sts just cast on, K8 sts of right front from st holder; across 22 sts of one sleeve work K7, (K2tog) 4 times, K7; K22 sts of back from st holder; across 22 sts of 2nd sleeve work K7, (K2tog) 4 times, K7; K8 sts of left front from st holder and cast on 4 sts at end of this row. (82 sts)
Starting with a P row, work 31 rows in st st, so ending with a P row.
*Next row (RS) K to 4 centre sts, (K2tog) twice to dec 2 sts at centre of hood, K to end.
Next row P to 4 centre sts, (P2tog) twice, P to end.*
Rep from * to * 4 times more. (62 sts)
K one row.
P one row. Cast off.

TOGGLES (MAKE 6)

With 3¼ mm needles and beige, cast on 8 sts.
Starting with a K row, work 6 rows in st st.
Cast off.

FINISHING

Join raglan sleeve seams, then join side and sleeve seams. Fold cast-off edge of hood in half and join hood seam.
Hems Fold hem of sleeves to WS along foldline (P row) and sew in place. Fold the hem of coat, the neck edge facing and the top of pockets to WS in same way and sew in place.
  Fold first 4 sts along centre edge of right and left fronts to WS and sew in place. Fold 4 sts along hood edge to WS and sew in place.
Pockets Sew one pocket to each front 2.5 cm (1 in) from side seam and 4 cm (1½ in) up from bottom of coat.
Toggles Cut six 2.5 cm (1 in) lengths from plastic drinking straw. Sew cast-off edge of one toggle to cast-on edge, enclosing one piece of straw while stitching. Sew tog each end of toggle so that straw is completely enclosed. Make rem five toggles in same way.
  Make three twisted cords (see page 13) each 12 cm (4¾ in) long. Sewing both ends of each cord tog to coat 3 cm (1¼ in) from folded centre front edge of *right front for Alice* and *left front for Andrew*, sew first cord 2 cm (¾ in) down from neck edge, the second 2.5 cm (1 in) from the first and the third 2.5 cm (1 in) from the second. Sew centre of one toggle to top of ends of each of three cords. Sew rem three toggles to opposite front 4 cm (1½ in) from folded edge to correspond with first three toggles.

SCARF AND MITTENS

SCARF

Cast on 16 sts.
1st rib row *K1, P1, rep from * to end.
Rep last row until scarf measures 54 cm (21¼ in) from cast-on edge. Cast off in rib.

MITTENS (make 2)

Cast on 38 sts.
Work 5 rows in K1, P1 rib as for scarf.
Next row (eyelet row) *Yfwd, K2tog, rep from * to end. (38 sts)
Starting with a K row, work 14 rows in st st, so ending with a P row.

Left: *Detail of back of Alice's duffle coat, pompon hat and scarf*

Next row (K2tog) 19 times. (19 sts)
P one row. Cast off.

FINISHING
Scarf fringe Wrap matching yarn 15 times
round a 4 cm (1½ in) piece of card. Cut loops
along one end of card. Fold one strand in half,
insert 2.5 mm crochet hook through first cast-
off st at end of scarf and draw folded end of
strand through edge of scarf, then draw cut
ends through loop on hook and pull tightly.

Using rem strands, work fringe evenly along
cast-off edge in same way. Then work fringe
along cast-on edge in same way. Trim ends.
Mittens Fold one mitten in half with right sides
tog, join row ends and top (cast-off edge) of
mitten. Turn right side out.

Make a 35 cm (13¾ in) long twisted cord (see
page 13) and thread it through the eyelet holes.
Finish second mitten in same way.

ALICE'S POMPON HAT

TO MAKE
With 3¼ mm needles, cast on 100 sts.

Work 17 rows in K1, P1 rib as for scarf.
Change to 4 mm needles.
Starting with a K row, work 8 rows in st st, so
ending with a P row.
Next row (RS) *K3, K2tog, rep from * to end.
(80 sts)
Starting with a P row, work 7 rows in st st.
Next row (RS) *K2, K2tog, rep from * to end.
(60 sts)
Starting with a P row, work 7 rows in st st.
Next row (RS) *K1, K2tog, rep from * to end.
(40 sts)
P one row.
Next row (K2tog) 20 times. (20 sts)
P one row.
Next row (K2tog) 10 times. (10 sts)
Break off yarn leaving a long loose end. Using a
blunt-ended needle, thread loose end through
all 10 sts on needle, pull yarn to gather
tightly, then fasten off.

FINISHING
With right sides tog, join hat seam (row ends).
Turn right side out and turn up ribbing to RS.
Make a 4 cm (1½ in) pompon (see pages 11-12)
and sew to top of hat.

BABY DOLL

♥ ♥

This lovable baby doll with removable hat, jacket, pants and bootees, is crying out to be dressed and undressed, cuddled and cared for – a sure favourite with any youngster who takes pleasure in parent/child role-play.

MATERIALS FOR BABY DOLL

- Double knitting yarn: 50 g pink for arms, legs, body and head, 40 g mid-blue for jacket, hat and bootees, 25 g light blue for pants
- Small amounts of double knitting yarn in black for eyes, yellow for hair and reddish-pink for nose and mouth
- Pair each of 3¼ mm (old size 10) and 4 mm (old size 8) knitting needles *or size to obtain correct tension*
- Good quality washable stuffing
- Red pencil for cheeks
- 60 cm (23½ in) of 5 mm (¼ in) wide elastic for pants
- Two 11 mm (⅜ in) buttons and two snap fasteners for jacket

SIZE Baby Doll measures approx 30.5 cm (12 in) in height, when worked in recommended tension

TENSION FOR DOLL 27 sts and 38 rows to 10 cm (4 in) measured over st st and worked on 3¼ mm needles

TENSION FOR CLOTHES 24 sts and 32 rows to 10 cm (4 in) measured over st st and worked on 4 mm needles
Check your tension before beginning and change needle size if necessary.

DOLL

BODY AND HEAD
With 3¼ mm needles and pink, cast on 56 sts.
Starting with a K row, work 32 rows in st st for body, so ending with a P row.
NECK SHAPING
Next row (RS) (K2tog) 28 times. (28 sts)
P one row.
Next row K into front and back of each st. (56 sts)
Starting with a P row, work 27 rows more in st st, so ending with a P row.
Next row (RS) (K2tog) 28 times. (28 sts)
Next row (P2tog) 14 times. (14 sts)
Break off yarn leaving a long loose end.
Using a blunt-ended needle, thread loose end through all 14 sts on needle, pull yarn to gather tightly, then fasten off.

ARMS (make 2)
With 3¼ mm needles and pink, cast on 6 sts.
1st row (RS) K into front and back of first st, K to last st, K into front and back of last st.
2nd row P into front and back of first st, P to last st, P into front and back of last st.

Rep last 2 rows 3 times more. (22 sts)
Starting with a K row, work 16 rows in st st, so ending with a P row.
WRIST SHAPING
Next row (RS) (K2tog) 11 times. (11 sts)
P one row.
Next row K into front and back of each st. (22 sts)
Starting with a P row, work 7 rows in st st, so ending with a P row.
Next row (RS) (K2tog) 11 times. (11 sts)
Break off yarn leaving a long loose end and fasten off as for top of head.

LEGS (make 2)
With 3¼ mm needles and pink, cast on 24 sts.
**1st row (RS) K into front and back of each st. (48 sts)
Starting with a P row, work 13 rows in st st, so ending with a P row.
Next row (RS) K6, (K2tog) twice, (K3tog) 9 times, (K2tog) twice, K7. (26 sts)**
Starting with a P row, work 27 rows in st st.
Cast off.

EARS (make 2)
With 3¼ mm needles and pink, cast on 6 sts.
1st row (RS) K into front and back of each st. (12 sts)
Starting with a P row, work 3 rows in st st, so ending with a P row.
Next row (RS) (K2tog) 6 times. (6 sts)
Next row (WS) (P2tog) 3 times. (3 sts)
Break off yarn leaving a long loose end and fasten off as for top of head.

FINISHING
Body, head and legs Finish body and head, and legs, as for Nurse (see page 46), but using pink for all seams.
Arms Join arm seams (row ends) up to top

shaping. Turn arms right side out.

Stuff each arm firmly and sew cast-on edge and shaped edges of one arm to body just below neck, with seam facing body.

Ears With wrong sides tog, join row ends of ears from cast-off edge to cast-on edge. Do not stuff. Oversew cast-on edge every alternate st, pull yarn to gather tightly and fasten off.

With seam facing head, sew one ear to each side of head, catching down at centre of ear to make an indent at centre and to flatten ear.

Hair Using yellow yarn, wind yarn round four fingers 12 times. Tie loops together at centre with a separate length of bright yellow yarn. Sew tied section to centre of top of head and spread loops out in a circle.

Embroidery Using a single 'ply' of reddish-pink yarn, work a semi-circle in backstitch for mouth.

Using a single 'ply' of reddish-pink yarn, work a short horizontal straight st and work three times over same st for nose.

Embroider eyes with black yarn (see page 10). Colour cheeks with red pencil.

PANTS

TO MAKE

The 2 legs are worked separately and then joined at the top.

FIRST LEG

*With 4 mm needles and light blue, cast on 40 sts.
Starting with a K row, work 3 rows in st st, so ending with a K row.
K one row (WS) for foldline.
Starting with a K row, work 6 rows in st st, so ending with a P row.*
Break off yarn and slip sts onto a spare needle.

SECOND LEG

Rep from * to *. Do not break off yarn.

JOINING LEGS

With RS facing, K40 sts of second leg, then K40 sts of first leg from spare needle. (80 sts)
Starting with a P row, work 11 rows in st st, so ending with a P row.
Next row (rib row) *K1, P1, rep from * to end.
Rep last row once more.
K one row (WS) for waistband foldline.
Starting with a K row, work 2 rows in st st.
Cast off.

FINISHING

Join centre back seam (row ends) of pants from cast-off edge to point where legs were joined, then join each leg seam (row ends) separately.

Fold hem of pant legs to WS along foldline and sew in place, leaving a small opening. On each leg, insert elastic through opening and thread through leg. Trim elastic to fit doll snugly, sew ends tog and sew up opening.

Fold waistband to WS along foldline and sew in place, leaving a small opening. Insert elastic as for hems and sew up opening.

JACKET

SLEEVES (make 2)

With 4 mm needles and mid-blue, cast on 30 sts.
K 4 rows (garter st).
Starting with a P row, work 9 rows in st st, so ending with a P row.

RAGLAN SHAPING

Next row (RS) Cast off 3 sts, K to end. (27 sts)
Next row Cast off 3 sts, P to end. (24 sts)
*Next row K2, K2tog, K to last 4 sts, K2tog tbl, K2.
P one row.*
Rep from * to * 6 times more. (10 sts)
Break off yarn and slip sts onto a st holder.

BACK

With 4 mm needles and mid-blue, cast on 54 sts.
K 4 rows (garter st).
Starting with a P row, work 9 rows in st st, so ending with a P row.
Next row (RS) *K1, K2tog, rep from * to end. (36 sts)
P one row.

RAGLAN ARMHOLE SHAPING

Next row (RS) Cast off 3 sts, K to end. (33 sts)
Next row Cast off 3 sts, P to end. (30 sts)
Next row (RS) K2, K2tog, K to last 4 sts, K2tog, K2.
K one row.**
Rep from ** to ** 6 times more. (16 sts)
Break off yarn and slip sts onto a st holder.

LEFT FRONT

With 4 mm needles and mid-blue, cast on 27 sts.
K 4 rows (garter st).
Next row (WS) K2, P to end.
K one row.**
Rep from ** to ** 3 times more.
Next row (WS) K2, P to end.

Next row *K1, K2tog, rep from * to end.
  (18 sts)
Next row K2, P to end.
RAGLAN ARMHOLE SHAPING
Next row (RS) Cast off 3 sts, K to end. (15 sts)
Next row K2, P to end.
***Next row** (RS) K2, K2tog, K to end.
K one row.***
Rep from *** to *** 5 times more. (9 sts)
Next row (RS) K2, K2tog, K to end. (8 sts)
Next row (WS) Cast off 4 sts, K to end. (4 sts)
Break off yarn and slip sts onto a st holder.

RIGHT FRONT

With 4 mm needles and mid-blue, cast on
  27 sts.
K 4 rows (garter st).
****Next row** (WS) P to last 2 sts, K2.
K one row.**
Rep from ** to ** 3 times more.
Next row (WS) P to last 2 sts, K2.
Next row *K1, K2tog, rep from * to end.
  (18 sts)
Next row P to last 2 sts, K2.
K one row.
RAGLAN ARMHOLE SHAPING
Next row (WS) Cast off 3 sts, P to last 2 sts, K2.
  (15 sts)
***Next row** (RS) K to last 4 sts, K2tog, K2.
K one row.***
Rep from *** to *** 5 times more. (9 sts)
Next row (RS) Cast off 4 sts, K2tog, K2. (4 sts)
K one row. Do not break off yarn.

COLLAR

With 4 mm needles and mid-blue, and with RS
facing, K4 sts of right front, K10 sts of one
sleeve from st holder, K16 sts of back from st
holder, K10 sts of 2nd sleeve from st holder
and K4 sts of left front from st holder. (44 sts)
1st rib row *K1, P1, rep from * to end.
Rep last row 9 times. Cast off loosely in rib.

FINISHING

Join raglan sleeve seams, then side and sleeve
seams. Sew 2 snap fasteners to garter st yoke
on front opening Sew on 2 decorative buttons.

BOOTEES

TO MAKE
With 4 mm needles cast on 24 sts in mid-blue.

Work as for leg of doll from ** to **.
P one row.
Next row (eyelet row) *Yfwd, K2tog, rep from *
  to end. (26 sts)
P one row.
K 4 rows (garter st). Cast off loosely.
Make 2nd bootee in same way.

FINISHING

Join row ends and bottom of each bootee.
  Using mid-blue yarn, make two twisted cords
each 40 cm (15¾ in) long (see page 13).
Starting at centre front, thread a cord through
eyelet holes at top of each bootee.

HAT

MAIN PART
With 4 mm needles and mid-blue, cast on
  70 sts.
K 4 rows (garter st).
Starting with a P row, work 3 rows in st st, so
  ending with a P row.
Next row (RS) *K3, K2tog, rep from * to end.
  (56 sts)
Starting with a P row, work 3 rows in st st.
Next row (RS) *K2, K2tog, rep from * to end.
  (42 sts)
Starting with a P row, work 3 rows in st st.
Next row (RS) *K1, K2tog, rep from * to end.
  (28 sts)
Starting with a P row, work 3 rows in st st.
Next row (RS) (K2tog) 14 times. (14 sts)
Break off yarn leaving a long loose end. Using a
  blunt-ended needle, thread loose end through
  all 14 sts on needle, pull yarn to gather
  tightly, then fasten off.

EAR FLAPS (make 2)
With 4 mm needles and mid-blue, cast on
  10 sts.
K 2 rows (garter st).
Next row K2tog, K to last 2 sts, K2tog.
Rep last row twice more. (4 sts)
Next row (K2tog) twice. (2 sts)
K 50 rows for strap.
Next row K2tog.
Fasten off.

FINISHING

Join centre back seam (row ends) of hat. Sew
one ear flap to cast-on edge at each side of hat.

Baby Doll (undressed)

THE ROLEY POLEY KIDS

★ ☆

Ma and Pa Roley Poley have their work cut out keeping control of a riotous brood of seven tumbling tots, featured here in full party swing!

MATERIALS FOR ROLEY POLEY KIDS

· Small amounts of double knitting yarn for each doll in pink for head, black for eyes and feet, red for nose and mouth, three contrasting colours (for upper body, lower body and hat), contrasting colour for jacket (optional), brown and light yellow for belt and buckle (optional), and chosen colour for hair
· Pair of 3¼ mm (old size 10) knitting needles *or size to obtain correct tension*
· Good quality washable stuffing
· Red pencil for cheeks

ROLEY POLEY KIDS

SIZE Each Roley Poley Kid measures approx 14 cm (5½ in) in height, when worked in recommended tension

TENSION 27 sts and 38 rows to 10 cm (4 in) measured over st st and worked on 3¼ mm needles
Check your tension before beginning and change needle size if necessary.

BASIC DOLL

BODY AND HEAD

Note: There is one basic doll pattern for all the Roley Poley Kids. By altering the type of clothing and hair and by changing colours various characters are created.

The following is the body and head for all the dolls without belts. (To work a doll with a belt and buckle refer to 'Belts' below.)

With colour for lower body, cast on 25 sts.

1st row (RS) K into front and back of each st. (50 sts)

Starting with a P row, work 14 rows in st st, so ending with a K row.

K one row (WS).

Break off lower body colour and change to colour for upper body.

**Starting with a K row, work 8 rows in st st, so ending with a P row.

NECK SHAPING

Next row (RS) (K2tog) 25 times. (25 sts)

P one row.

Break off upper body colour and change to pink for head.

K one row.

Next row (WS) *P1, P into front and back of
  next st, rep from * to last st, P1. (37 sts)
Starting with a K row, work 16 rows more in
  st st, so ending with a P row.
Next row (RS) (K2tog) 18 times, K1. (19 sts)
Next row (P2tog) 9 times, P1. (10 sts)
Break off yarn leaving a long loose end.
Using a blunt-ended needle, thread loose end
  through all 10 sts on needle, pull yarn to
  gather tightly, then fasten off.**

ARMS (make 2)
With pink, cast on 10 sts.
Starting with a K row, work 18 rows in st st, so
  ending with a P row.
Next row (RS) (K2tog) 5 times. (5 sts)
Break off yarn leaving a long loose end. Using a
  blunt-ended needle, thread loose end through
  all 5 sts on needle, pull yarn to gather tightly,
  then fasten off.

FEET (make 2)
With black (or desired colour for shoe), cast on
  10 sts.
Starting with a K row, work 10 rows in st st, so
  ending with a P row.
Next row (RS) (K2tog) 5 times. (5 sts)
Starting with a P row, work 5 rows in st st, so
  ending with a P row.
Next row (RS) K into front and back of each st.
  (10 sts)
Starting with a P row, work 10 rows in st st,
  so ending with a K row.
Cast off purlwise.

FINISHING
Body and head Join centre back seam (row
ends) of body and head, using matching yarn
for each section and leaving cast-on edge open.
Turn right side out.
  Stuff body and head firmly. Oversew cast-on
edge every alternate st, pull yarn to gather
tightly and fasten off.
  To shape neck wrap a length of upper-body
colour yarn twice round the neck between the
dec and inc rows. Pull yarn tightly to gather
neck, knot at centre back neck and sew ends
into neck.
Arms Join arm seams (row ends), leaving cast-
on edge open. Turn arms right side out.
  Stuff each arm firmly and sew top tog,
keeping seam at centre.
  Do not sew the arms to the body until the

sleeves have been completed.
Feet With wrong sides tog, fold one foot in half
between the dec and inc rows. Join row ends
and join cast-off edge to cast-on edge. (Do not
stuff feet.)
  Sew other foot tog in same way. Sew cast-on/
cast-off edge of each foot to bottom of body.
Hair Work hair before sewing on hats. See
'Finishing' for clothes.
Embroidery Using a single 'ply' of red yarn,
work a V-shaped mouth.
  Using a single 'ply' of red yarn, work a short
horizontal straight st and work twice over same
st for nose.
  Using black yarn, embroider eyes (see
page 10). Colour cheeks with red pencil.

CLOTHES

LONG SLEEVES (make 2)
With upper body colour (or jacket colour), cast
  on 14 sts.
Starting with a K row, work 14 rows in st st, so
  ending with a P row.
Next row (RS) (K2tog) 7 times. (7 sts)
Break off yarn leaving a long loose end.
Using a blunt-ended needle, thread loose end
  through all 7 sts on needle, pull yarn to gather
  tightly, then fasten off.

SHORT SLEEVES (make 2)
With upper body colour (or jacket colour), cast
  on 14 sts.
Starting with a K row, work 6 rows in st st,
  so ending with a P row.
Next row (RS) (K2tog) 7 times. (7 sts)
Break off yarn leaving a long loose end.
Using a blunt-ended needle, thread loose end
  through all 7 sts on needle, pull yarn to gather
  tightly, then fasten off.

PUFFED SLEEVES (make 2)
With upper body colour (or jacket colour), cast
  on 12 sts.
1st row (RS) K into front and back of each st.
  (24 sts)
Starting with a P row, work 7 rows in st st,
  so ending with a P row.
Next row (RS) (K2tog) 12 times. (12 sts)
Next row (P2tog) 6 times. (6 sts)
Break off yarn leaving a long loose end and
  fasten off as for long sleeve.

TROUSER STRAPS (make 2)
With lower body colour, cast on 30 sts.
K one row. Cast off.

DUNGAREE BIB
With lower body colour, cast on 14 sts.
Starting with a K row, work 8 rows in st st.
Cast off.

DUNGAREE STRAPS (make 2)
With dungaree colour, cast on 20 sts.
Cast off.

BELT
For body and head with knit-in belt work as
  follows:
With lower body colour, cast on 25 sts.
1st row (RS) K into front and back of each st.
  (50 sts)
Starting with a P row, work 12 rows in st st, so
  ending with a K row.
Break off lower body colour and change to
  brown for belt.
P 2 rows.
K one row.

Break off brown and change to upper body
  colour.
Complete as for body and head of basic doll
  (see pages 36-38) from ** to **.

JACKET
With jacket colour, cast on 50 sts.
K 2 rows (garter st).
***Next row** (WS) K2, P46, K2.
K one row.*
Rep from * to * 4 times more.
Next row (WS) K2, P46, K2.
Next row (K2tog) 25 times. (25 sts)
K one row.
Cast off.

GIRL'S HAT
With hat colour, cast on 76 sts.
K 2 rows (garter st).
Next row (WS) *K1, K2tog, rep from * to last st,
  K1. (51 sts)
Next row *K1, K2tog, rep from * to end.
  (34 sts)
Starting with a P row, work 11 rows in st st,
  so ending with a P row.

Right: *Working a buttonhole stitch buckle on belt*

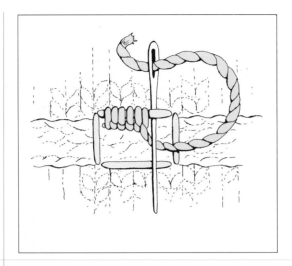

Next row (RS) *K2, K2tog, rep from * to last 2 sts, K2. (26 sts)
P one row.
Next row (K2tog) 13 times. (13 sts)
P one row.
Break off yarn leaving a long loose end and fasten off as for long sleeve.

BOY'S HAT

With hat colour, cast on 76 sts.
K 2 rows (garter st).
Next row (WS) (K2tog) 38 times. (38 sts)
Starting with a K row, work 8 rows in st st, so ending with a P row.
Next row (RS) (K2tog) 19 times. (19 sts)
Break off yarn leaving a long loose end and fasten off as for long sleeve.

FINISHING

Jacket If doll has a jacket, sew jacket to doll before arms. Sew cast-off edge of jacket to body along neckline with centre of jacket at centre back of body.
Sleeves and arms Join sleeve seams (row ends). Turn right side out.
Insert arms into sleeves with seams lined up, then sew ends of arms to sleeves. With sleeve seams facing body, sew one sleeve to each side of body just below neck (stitching through jacket if there is one).
Dungaree bib Sew cast-on edge of bib to front of body along P row at waistline, then stitch other three sides in place. If desired, embroider a cross in centre of bib in contrasting colour.
Sew one end of each dungaree strap to corner of bib and the other end to centre back on P row at waistline, stitching all along strap.

Trouser straps Sew one end of each strap to back on P row at waistline so that straps are about 2 cm (¾ in) apart. Cross straps at back and take over shoulders to front, so that straps cover P row at waistline on front. Sew in place all along strap.
Embroider button on straps at front ends, using a contrasting colour.
Buckle Using light yellow, work a buttonhole stitch buckle on each knitted belt (as shown in the illustration).
Tied belt Using a contrasting colour and starting at centre front, work a running st along waistline of lower body just below P row. Tie a bow at centre front and trim ends.
Boy's hat and hair Join row ends of hat and turn right side out. Sew hat to top of boy's head all along first row after garter st brim. Using chosen hair colour, work a few loops coming out from under hat at centre of forehead.
Girl's plaits Using chosen hair colour, make a 21.5 cm (8½ in) plait tied at each end with a contrasting bow, using seven strands of yarn for each of three sections of plait. Sew centre of plait to top of head.
For fringe loosely wrap yarn about 24 times round a 6 cm (2½ in) piece of card. Slip looped yarn carefully off card, keeping it folded in half. Wrap a separate length of yarn round centre of looped yarn, pull tightly and knot. Sew tied section to top of head and push both looped bunches forward, spreading them out to cover the forehead.
Short curly hair Using chosen hair colour, loosely wrap yarn about 26 times round a 8.5 cm (3¼ in) piece of card. Slip looped yarn carefully off card, keeping it folded in half. Wrap a separate length of yarn round looped yarn 3 cm (1¼ in) from one end, pull tightly and knot. Sew tied section to top of head so that short loops hang down over forehead to form fringe. Separate longer loops in half and push each bunch forward to side of head.
Short straight hair Using chosen hair colour, cut about thirty-two 19 cm (7½ in) lengths of yarn. Holding the lengths tog, fold in half. Wrap a separate length of yarn round the folded strands 3 cm (1¼ in) from the fold, pull tightly and knot. Sew the tied section to the top of the head so that the loops hang down over the forehead to form a fringe. Separate longer strands in half and push each bunch forward to the side of the head. Trim ends.

Hair bunches Using chosen hair colour, cut about twenty-two 18 cm (7 in) lengths of yarn. Wrap a separate length of yarn round centre of strands, pull tightly and knot. Sew the tied section to the top of the head so that the loose ends hang down over the sides of the head. Tie a contrasting bow round the loose strands at each side of the head above the shoulders. Sew tied bow to head. Trim hair ends.

For bunches with fringe work as for straight hair but cut 21 cm (8¼ in) lengths of yarn.

Girl's hat Join row ends of hat and turn right side out. Sew the hat to top of girl's head all along first row after garter st brim.

* *

MATERIALS FOR MA ROLEY POLEY

- Double knitting yarn: 50 g pink for head and arms, 30 g yellow for blouse, 30 g blue for dungarees, 25 g dark brown for hair, 20 g dark pink for hat
- Small amounts of double knitting yarn in black for feet and eyes, light blue for trim and red for nose and mouth
- Pair of 3¼ mm (old size 10) knitting needles *or size to obtain correct tension*
- Good quality washable stuffing
- Red pencil for cheeks

MA ROLEY POLEY

SIZE Ma Roley Poley measures approx 24 cm (9½ in) in height, when worked in recommended tension

TENSION 27 sts and 38 rows to 10 cm (4 in) measured over st st and worked on 3¼ mm needles

Check your tension before beginning and change needle size if necessary.

BASIC DOLL

BODY AND HEAD
With blue, cast on 25 sts.

1st row (RS) K into front and back of each st. (50 sts)

2nd row Purl.

3rd row (RS) K into front and back of each st. (100 sts)

Starting with a P row, work 28 rows in st st, so ending with a K row.

K one row (WS).

P one row (RS).

Break off blue and change to yellow.

Starting with a P row, work 17 rows in st st, so ending with a P row.

NECK SHAPING
Next row (RS) (K2tog) 50 times. (50 sts)

P one row.

Break off yellow and change to pink for head.

K one row.

Next row (WS) *P1, P into front and back of next st, rep from * to end. (75 sts)

Starting with a K row, work 32 rows more in st st, so ending with a P row.

Next row (RS) (K2tog) 37 times, K1. (38 sts)

Next row (P2tog) 19 times. (19 sts)

Break off yarn leaving a long loose end.

Using a blunt-ended needle, thread loose end through all 19 sts on needle, pull yarn to gather tightly, then fasten off.

ARMS (make 2)
With pink, cast on 20 sts.

Starting with a K row, work 36 rows in st st, so ending with a P row.

Next row (RS) (K2tog) 10 times. (10 sts)

Break off yarn leaving a long loose end and fasten off as for top of head.

FEET (make 2)
With black, cast on 20 sts.

Starting with K row, work 20 rows in st st, so ending with a P row.

Next row (RS) (K2tog) 10 times. (10 sts)

Starting with P row, work 10 rows in st st, so ending with a K row.

Next row (WS) P into front and back of each st. (20 sts)

Starting with K row, work 20 rows in st st.

Cast off.

FINISHING
Finish as for Roley Poley Kids, but work a running st around neck and gather to shape neck.

Do not sew arms to body until sleeves have been completed.

Embroidery Using red yarn, work a V-shape for the mouth.

Using red yarn, work a short horizontal straight st and work twice over same st for the nose.

Using black yarn, embroider eyes (see instructions on page 10).

Colour cheeks with red pencil.

Hair Loosely wrap dark brown yarn about 70 times round a 23 cm (9 in) piece of card. Slip looped yarn carefully off card, keeping it folded in half. Wrap a separate length of yarn round looped yarn 10 cm (4 in) from one end, pull tightly and knot. Sew tied section to centre back of head so that short loops hang down over forehead to form fringe.

Spread longer loops out over the back and sides of head.

CLOTHES

SLEEVES (make 2)
With yellow, cast on 28 sts.
Starting with a K row, work 28 rows in st st, so ending with a P row.
Next row (RS) (K2tog) 14 times. (14 sts)
Next row (P2tog) 7 times. (7 sts)

Break off yarn leaving a long loose end.
Using a blunt-ended needle, thread loose end through all 7 sts on needle, pull yarn to gather tightly, then fasten off.

DUNGAREE BIB
With blue, cast on 28 sts.
Starting with a K row, work 16 rows in st st.
Cast off.

DUNGAREE STRAPS (make 2)
With blue, cast on 40 sts.
K 2 rows (garter st).
Cast off.

Below: Ma and Pa Roley Poley

MA'S HAT

With dark pink, cast on 152 sts.
K 3 rows (garter st).
Next row *K1, K2tog, rep from * to last 2 sts, K2. (102 sts)
K 3 rows.
Next row *K1, K2tog, rep from * to end. (68 sts)
Starting with a P row, work 23 rows in st st, so ending with a P row.
Next row (RS) *K2, K2tog, rep from * to end. (51 sts)
P one row.
Next row (K2tog) 25 times, K1. (26 sts)

Next row (P2tog) 13 times. (13 sts)
Break off yarn leaving a long loose end and fasten off as for sleeve.

FINISHING

Sleeves and arms Finish and sew to body as for Roley Poley Kids.
Dungaree bib Sew bib and straps to body as for Roley Poley Kids.
Using light blue, embroider a chain-st cross in centre of bib.
Hat Join row ends of hat and turn right side out. Sew hat to top of head all along first row after garter st brim.

MATERIALS FOR PA ROLEY POLEY

- Double knitting yarn: 50 g pink for head and arms, 30 g each white and dark green for upper and lower body, 30 g red for jacket, 20 g mid-blue for hat
- Small amounts of double knitting yarn in black for feet and eyes, yellow for hair and red for nose and mouth
- Pair of 3¼ mm (old size 10) knitting needles *or size to obtain correct tension*
- Good quality washable stuffing
- Red pencil for cheeks

PA ROLEY POLEY

SIZE As for Ma Roley Poley

TENSION As for Ma Roley Poley

BASIC DOLL

BODY AND HEAD

Work as for Ma Roley Poley, but using dark green for lower and white for upper body.

ARMS AND FEET

Work as for Ma Roley Poley.

FINISHING

Finish as for Ma Roley Poley (except for hair). Do not sew arms to body until sleeves and jacket have been completed.
Hair Loosely wrap yellow yarn about 12 times round a 13 cm (5 in) piece of card. Slip looped yarn carefully off card, keeping it folded in half. Wrap a separate length of yarn round centre of the looped yarn, pull tightly and knot. Sew tied section to top of head and push both bunches forward toward front of head, spreading evenly along forehead. (Hat will hold hair in place.)

CLOTHES

SLEEVES

Work as for Ma Roley Poley, but using red yarn instead of yellow to match the jacket.

JACKET

With red, cast on 100 sts.
K 4 rows (garter st).
***Next row** (WS) K4, P92, K4.
K one row.*
Rep from * to * 10 times more.
Next row (WS) K4, P92, K4.
Next row (K2tog) 50 times. (50 sts)
K 3 rows.
Cast off.

PA'S HAT

With mid-blue, cast on 152 sts.
K 4 rows (garter st).
Next row (K2tog) 76 times. (76 sts)
Starting with a K row, work 16 rows in st st, so ending with a P row.
Next row (K2tog) 38 times. (38 sts)
Next row (P2tog) 19 times. (19 sts)
Break off yarn leaving a long loose end.
Using a blunt-ended needle, thread loose end through all 19 sts on needle, pull yarn to gather tightly, then fasten off.

FINISHING

Jacket sleeves Join sleeve seams (row ends). Turn right side out.
Insert arms into sleeves with seams lined up, then sew ends of arms to sleeves. With sleeve seams facing body, sew one sleeve to each side of body, stitching through jacket.
Hat Join row ends of hat and turn right side out. Sew hat to top of head all along first row after garter st brim.

CASUALTY WARD

It's another busy day on the ward for the kindly Nurse, bandaging sore heads and attending to the latest casualty, Bertie Bear.

MATERIALS FOR NURSE

- Double knitting yarn: 50 g pink for arms, legs, body and head, 40 g white for apron, hat and pants, 50 g blue for dress, 25 g yellow for hair
- Small amounts of double knitting yarn in black for eyes and shoes and red for mouth and cross
- Pair of 3¼ mm (old size 10) knitting needles *or size to obtain correct tension*
- Good quality washable stuffing
- Red pencil for cheeks

NURSE

SIZE Nurse measures approx 30.5 cm (12 in) in height, when worked in recommended tension

TENSION 27 sts and 38 rows to 10 cm (4 in) measured over st st and worked on 3¼ mm needles
Check your tension before beginning and change needle size if necessary.

DOLL

BODY AND HEAD
With white, cast on 40 sts.
K 3 rows (garter st).
Starting with a P row, work 12 rows in st st, so ending with a K row.
K one row (WS).
Break off white and change to pink.
Starting with a K row, work 16 rows in st st, so ending with a P row.

NECK SHAPING
Next row (RS) (K2tog) 20 times. (20 sts)
P one row.
Next row K into front and back of each st. (40 sts)
Starting with a P row, work 29 rows more in st st, so ending with a P row.
Next row (RS) (K2tog) 20 times. (20 sts)
Next row (P2tog) 10 times. (10 sts)
Break off yarn leaving a long loose end.
Using a blunt-ended needle, thread loose end through all 10 sts on needle, pull yarn to gather tightly, then fasten off.

ARMS (make 2)
With pink, cast on 8 sts.
1st row (RS) K into front and back of each st. (16 sts)
Starting with a P row, work 41 rows in st st.
Cast off all 16 sts.

Nurse

each arm open. Turn arms right side out.

Stuff each arm firmly and oversew top edge tog, keeping seam at centre.

To shape wrist wrap a length of pink yarn once round arm about 13 rows from gathered end. Pull yarn tightly to gather wrist, knot at seam and sew ends into seam.

Do not sew arms to body until dress has been completed.

Hair Loosely wrap yellow yarn about 50 times round a 15 cm (6 in) piece of card. Slip looped yarn carefully off card, keeping it folded in half. Wrap a separate length of yellow yarn round the centre of the looped yarn, pull tightly and knot. Sew the tied section to the centre of the back of the head and evenly spread out the loops to cover the head. Sew the hair in place by working backstitch along the looped ends all round head (these ends will be covered by a row of bunched curls).

For bunched curls, loosely wrap yellow yarn about 25 times round a 3 cm (1¼ in) piece of card. Slip off card and tie at centre as for main hair. Make 12 more bunches in the same way. Sew curls all round head covering loop ends already stitched in place.

Embroidery Work mouth, eyes and nose as for Goldilocks (see page 97), and colour cheeks with red pencil.

DRESS

MAIN PART

With blue, cast on 100 sts.

K 4 rows (garter st).

Starting with a P row, work 23 rows in st st, so ending with a P row.

Next row (RS) *K1, K2tog, rep from * to last st, K1. (67 sts)

Starting with a P row, work 17 rows in st st, so ending with a P row.

Next row (RS) *K2tog, rep from * to last st, K1. (34 sts)

K 2 rows. Cast off.

SLEEVES (make 2)

With blue, cast on 20 sts.

K one row.

Next row (RS) K into front and back of each st. (40 sts)

Starting with a P row, work 13 rows in st st, so ending with a P row.

LEGS (make 2)

With black, cast on 18 sts.

1st row (RS) K into front and back of each st. (36 sts)

Starting with a P row, work 9 rows in st st, so ending with a P row.

Next row (RS) K6, (K3tog) 8 times, K6. (20 sts)

K one row (WS).

Break off black and change to pink for leg.

Starting with a K row, work 30 rows in st st. Cast off.

FINISHING

Body and head Join centre back seam (row ends) of body and head, using matching yarn for each section and leaving cast-on edge of body open. Turn right side out.

Stuff body and head firmly. Oversew cast-on edge of body tog, keeping seam at centre back.

To shape neck wrap a length of pink yarn twice round the neck between the dec and inc rows. Pull yarn tightly to gather neck, knot at centre back neck and sew ends into neck.

Legs Join lower edge and centre back (row ends) of each leg, using matching yarn for each section and leaving top edge of each leg open. Turn legs right side out.

Stuff each leg firmly and oversew top edge tog, keeping seam at centre back. Sew legs to lower edge of body.

Arms Join arm seams (row ends), leaving top of

Next row (RS) (K2tog) 20 times. (20 sts)
P one row.
Next row (K2tog) 10 times. (10 sts)
Break off yarn leaving a long loose end.
Using a blunt-ended needle, thread loose end
    through all 10 sts on needle, pull yarn to
    gather tightly, then fasten off.

FINISHING
Main part Put main part of dress on doll and
join centre back seam (row ends).
Sleeves Join sleeve seams (row ends). Turn
right side out.
   Insert arms into sleeves with seams lined up,
then sew ends of arms to sleeves. With sleeve
seams facing body, sew one sleeve to each side
of body just below neck, stitching through dress.

APRON

TO MAKE
With white, cast on 40 sts.
K 4 rows (garter st).
*Next row** (WS) K2, P36, K2.
K one row.*
Rep from * to * 7 times more.
Next row (WS) K10, P20, K10.
K one row.
BIB SHAPING
Next row (WS) Cast off 10 sts knitwise, P to last

10 sts, cast off last 10 sts knitwise.
With RS facing, rejoin yarn and K one row.
Next row (WS) K2, P16, K2.
K one row.**
Rep from ** to ** 3 times more.
K 2 rows.
Cast off knitwise.

FINISHING
Sew top (cast-off edge) of bib to front of dress
1.5 cm (½ in) below neckline. Then sew corners
of apron waistline to dress under arms.
   Using red, embroider a cross at centre of bib.

NURSE'S CAP

TO MAKE
With white, cast on 30 sts.
K 4 rows (garter st).
*Next row** (WS) K2, P26, K2.
K one row.*
Rep from * to * 3 times more.
K 4 rows.
Cast off.

FINISHING
Sew cast-off edge of cap to bunched curls at
top of head.
   Using red yarn, embroider a cross at centre of
cap above garter st edge at bottom of cap.

MATERIALS FOR BERTIE BEAR
· Double knitting yarn:
   40 g light camel for
   body, head, arms and
   legs and small
   amounts in medium
   camel for bottom of
   feet, black for features
   and white for eye
   patch
·Pair of 3¼ mm (old
   size 10) knitting
   needles *or size to
   obtain correct tension*

BERTIE BEAR

SIZE Bertie Bear measures approx 16.5 cm
(6½ in) in height seated (including ears), when
worked in recommended tension

TENSION As for Nurse

BEAR

BODY AND HEAD
Work body and head as for Daddy and Mummy
   Bear (see page 98), but use light camel.

ARMS (make 2)
With light camel, cast on 10 sts.
1st row (RS) K into front and back of each st.
   (20 sts)

Starting with a P row, work 5 rows in st st, so
   ending with a P row.
WRIST SHAPING
Next row (RS) (K2tog) twice, K12, (K2tog)
   twice. (16 sts)
Starting with a P row, work 17 rows in st st for
   arm, so ending with a P row.
Next row (RS) (K2tog) 8 times. (8 sts)
P one row. Cast off.

LEGS (make 2)
With medium camel, cast on 6 sts.
1st row (RS) K into front and back of each st.
   (12 sts)
P one row.
Next row K into front and back of each st.
   (24 sts)
P one row.
Break off medium camel and change to light camel.

Right: *Bertie Bear*

Starting with a K row, work 6 rows in st st, so ending with a P row.

Next row (RS) (K2tog) twice, K16, (K2tog) twice. (20 sts)

Starting with a P row, work 17 rows in st st, so ending with a P row.

Next row (RS) (K2tog) 10 times. (10 sts)

P one row. Cast off.

EARS (make 2)

With light camel, cast on 14 sts.

Starting with a K row, work 10 rows in st st.

Next row (RS) (K2tog) twice, K6, (K2tog) twice. (10 sts)

Starting with a P row, work 9 rows in st st. Cast off.

EYE PATCH

With white, cast on 10 sts.

Work 74 rows in st st. Cast off.

FINISHING

Body and head Finish and stuff body and head as for Daddy and Mummy Bear (see page 98).

Legs Join leg seams (row ends), leaving cast-off end open. Oversew cast-on edge every alternate st, pull yarn to gather tightly and fasten off. Turn legs right side out.

Stuff each leg firmly, but only from foot to within 2.5 cm (1 in) from top of leg, then over-sew top edge tog, keeping seam at centre.

Sew unstuffed section of each leg to bottom of bear's body, with leg seam facing upwards and with 2.5 cm (1 in) of each leg under body and legs in seated position.

Arms Join arm seams (row ends) and bottom of arms, leaving top of each arm open. Turn arms right side out.

Stuff each arm firmly and oversew top edge tog.

Sew arms to body just below neck.

Ears Fold one ear in half along dec row, with right sides tog. Join side seam (row ends) on first side of ear and when fold is reached, secure yarn but do not break off. Now work a running st along fold, pull yarn to gather slightly and secure yarn, then continue seam down other side of ear. Turn ear right side out.

Do not stuff. Oversew cast-on and cast-off edges tog. Sew other ear tog in same way. Sew ears to top of head.

Embroidery Using a single 'ply' of black double knitting yarn, work a satin st triangle for nose. Still using black, work a short vertical straight st from centre of nose to centre of mouth and work a V-shaped mouth.

Using black yarn, make eyes (see page 10).

Wrap eye patch bandage around left ear and over left eye. Wrap a length of white yarn around ends of bandage between ears at top of head and secure, then sew bandage to head.

MATERIALS FOR MEDICAL EQUIPMENT

· Small amounts of 4-ply knitting yarn in white for bandage and in light grey and black for scissors
· Small amounts of double knitting yarn in white, black and light grey for stethoscope
· Pair each of 2¾ mm (old size 12) and 3¼ mm (old size 10) knitting needles *or size to obtain correct tension*
· Piece of thin plastic for the scissors (see Finishing)

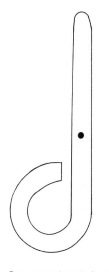

Cut two scissor pieces
from soft plastic

MEDICAL EQUIPMENT

TENSION 27 sts and 38 rows to 10 cm (4 in) measured over st st and worked on 3¼ mm needles, using double knitting yarn
18 sts and 26 rows to 5 cm (2 in) measured over st st and worked on 2¾ mm needles, using 4-ply yarn

BANDAGE

TO MAKE
With 2¾ mm needles and white 4-ply, cast on 6 sts.
Starting with a K row (and knitting first and last st of every P row), work in st st until bandage measures 33 cm (13 in) from cast-on edge.
Cast off.

FINISHING
Roll up bandage with knit side on outside, leaving 5 cm (2 in) unrolled. Stitch through roll twice to keep it from unrolling.

SCISSORS

TO MAKE
With 2¾ mm needles and light grey 4-ply, cast on 6 sts.
Starting with a K row, work 46 rows in st st, so ending with a P row.
Next row (RS) (K2tog) 3 times. (3 sts)
Break off yarn leaving a long loose end.
Using a blunt-ended needle, thread loose end through all 3 sts on needle, pull yarn to gather tightly, then fasten off.
Make a second piece in the same way.

FINISHING
Using a soft plastic ice cream container, cut two pieces of plastic in a scissor shape as shown in the diagram.
   With wrong sides tog, join row ends of each scissor piece, leaving cast-on edges open. Slip point of one piece of plastic into open end of one of scissor pieces, then push knitting up piece of plastic, easing it round the handle. Oversew cast-on edge to side of scissor to complete handle.
   Complete other scissor piece in same way.
   Using black yarn, sew the two scissor pieces tog in position.

STETHOSCOPE

NECK CORD
With 3¼ mm needles and black double knitting yarn, cast on 42 sts.
Starting with a K row, work 6 rows in st st.
Cast off.

CONNECTOR CORD
Work as for neck cord but cast on only 18 sts.
Cast off.

EAR PIECES (make 2)
With 3¼ mm needles and white double knitting yarn, cast on 4 sts.
1st row (RS) K into front and back of each st. (8 sts)
Starting with a P row, work 3 rows in st st, so ending with a P row.
Next row (RS) (K2tog) 4 times. (4 sts)
Break off yarn leaving a long loose end.
Using a blunt-ended needle, thread loose end through all 4 sts on needle, pull yarn to gather tightly, then fasten off.

LISTENING BELL
With 3¼ mm needles and grey double knitting yarn used double throughout, cast on 24 sts.
K one row.
Starting with a K row, work 4 rows in st st, so ending with a P row.
Next row (RS) (K2tog) 12 times. (12 sts)
P one row.
Next row (RS) (K2tog) 6 times. (6 sts)
Break off yarn leaving a long loose end.
Using a blunt-ended needle, thread loose end through all 6 sts on needle, pull yarn to gather tightly, then fasten off.

FINISHING
Starting at cast-off edge, roll up neck cord with knit side on outside. Sew down cast-on edge, pulling stitches while sewing to curve knitting.
   Roll up connector cord in same way and stitch, but do not curve.
   Join row ends of bell and turn right side out. Sew one end of connector cord to end of bell and other end to middle of neck cord.
   Oversew round three edges of one ear piece, place WS on one end of the neck cord, then pull to gather ear piece tightly round cord and sew firmly in place. Finish the other ear piece in the same way.

JOJO THE CLOWN

★ ★

Everybody loves a clown and JoJo is no exception. With his cheerful smile and wacky outfit, he is guaranteed to brighten up even the gloomiest winter day and provide children with hours of amusing 'circus' entertainment.

MATERIALS FOR JOJO THE CLOWN

· Double knitting yarn: 75 g pink for hands and head, 50 g white for legs and trim, 150 g red for hat and trousers, 50 g black for shoes, 50 g each green and light green for top, 25 g yellow for hair, small amount of mid-blue for trim
· Pair of 3¼ mm (old size 10) 36 cm (14 in) long knitting needles *or size to obtain correct tension*
· 750 g (1½ lbs) good quality washable stuffing
· Red pencil for cheeks

SIZE JoJo the Clown measures approx 53 cm (21 in) in height (including hat), when worked in recommended tension

TENSION 27 sts and 38 rows to 10 cm (4 in) measured over st st and worked on 3¼ mm needles
Check your tension before beginning and change needle size if necessary.

DOLL

LEGS, BODY AND HEAD
The 2 legs are worked separately and then joined at the top.

RIGHT LEG
*With black (for shoes), cast on 40 sts.
1st row (RS) K into front and back of each st. (80 sts)
Starting with a P row, work 21 rows in st st, so ending with a P row.*
Next row (RS) K8, (K2tog) 24 times, K24. (56 sts)
P one row.
Next row K6, (K2tog) 14 times, K22. (42 sts)
**Starting with a P row, work 7 rows in st st, so ending with a P row.
Break off black and change to white for leg.
Starting with a K row, work 36 rows more in st st, so ending with a P row.**
Break off yarn and slip sts onto a spare needle. This completes right leg.

LEFT LEG
Work as for right leg from * to *.
Next row (RS) K24, (K2tog) 24 times, K8. (56 sts)
P one row.
Next row K22, (K2tog) 14 times, K6. (42 sts)
Complete as for right leg from ** to **.
Break off yarn.

JOINING LEGS
With RS facing and with green, K42 sts of left leg, then K42 sts of right leg from spare needle. (84 sts)
Starting with a P row, work 3 rows in st st, so ending with a P row.
***With light green, work 4 rows in st st.
With green, work 4 rows in st st.***
Rep from *** to *** 4 times more.
With light green, work 4 rows more in st st.
Break off light green and continue with green.

NECK SHAPING
Next row (RS) K12, (K2tog) 10 times, K20, (K2tog) 10 times, K12. (64 sts)
Starting with a P row, work 3 rows in st st, so ending with a P row.
Break off green and change to pink for head.
K one row.
P one row.
Next row K16, K into front and back of next 32 sts, K16. (96 sts)
Starting with a P row, work 45 rows in st st, so ending with a P row.
Next row (K2tog) 48 times. (48 sts)
P one row.
Next row (K2tog) 24 times. (24 sts)
P one row.
Break off yarn leaving a long loose end. Using a blunt-ended needle, thread loose end through all 24 sts on needle, pull yarn to gather tightly, then fasten off.

ARMS (make 2)
With pink, cast on 20 sts.
1st row (RS) K into front and back of each st. (40 sts)
Starting with a P row, work 17 rows in st st, so ending with a P row.
Break off pink and change to green for sleeve.
Starting with a K row, work 4 rows in st st, so ending with a P row.

***With light green, work 4 rows in st st.
With green, work 4 rows in st st.***
Rep from *** to *** 4 times more.
Break off green and continue with light green.
Starting with a K row, work 2 rows more in
  st st, so ending with a P row.
Next row (RS) (K2tog) 20 times. (20 sts)
Cast off purlwise.

NOSE
With red, cast on 10 sts.
1st row (RS) K into front and back of each st.
  (20 sts)
Starting with a P row, work 9 rows in st st,
  so ending with a P row.
Next row (RS) (K2tog) 10 times. (10 sts)
Break off yarn leaving a long loose end and
  fasten off as for top of head.

FINISHING
Body and head With right sides tog, join centre
back seam (row ends) of body and head down
to leg division, using matching yarn for each
section.

Leave a small opening (for turning right side
out and stuffing), then join row ends of legs and
bottom of each foot. Turn right side out.

Stuff legs, body and head firmly, then sew
opening tog.

To shape neck, using a long length of pink
yarn, start at centre back neck and work running
st along first row of pink. Pull both ends tightly
to gather neck and knot at centre back. Then
wrap one end of yarn once round neck, pull,
knot at centre back of neck and sew the ends
into the neck.

Below: Detail of trouser patch

Arms With right sides tog and using pink for
hand and green for sleeve, join arm seams (row
ends) and bottom of hands, keeping seam in
centre and leaving top of each arm open. Turn
arms right side out.

Stuff each arm lightly (so that they can bend
slightly) and sew top tog. Sew top of one arm
to each side of body at neck.
Nose With right sides tog, join row ends of
nose. Turn right side out and stuff.

Oversew cast-on edge every alternate st, pull
yarn to gather tightly and fasten off.

Sew nose to face so that bottom of nose is
positioned 5.5 cm (2¼ in) up from neck.
Embroidery Using red yarn and working in
backstitch, work semi-circle for mouth, then
weave yarn in and out of backstitches back to
beginning and fasten off.

Using black yarn, embroider eyes (see
instructions given on page 10). Colour cheeks
with red pencil.
Hair Cut about one hundred and sixty 35.5 cm
(14 in) lengths of yellow yarn. Wrap a separate
length of yellow yarn round centre of strands,
pull tightly and knot.

Sew tied section to top of head so that loose
ends hang down over sides of head. Spread out
strands evenly to cover sides and back of head.

TROUSERS AND CUFFS

TROUSERS
The 2 legs are worked separately and then
  joined at the top.
FIRST LEG
*With red, cast on 80 sts.
K 3 rows (garter st).
Next row (RS) *K1, K into front and back of
  next st, rep from * to end. (120 sts)
Starting with a P row, work 27 rows in st st,
  so ending with a P row.*
Break off yarn and slip sts onto a spare needle.
SECOND LEG
Rep from * to * for second leg. Do not break
  off yarn.
JOINING LEGS
With RS facing, K120 sts of second leg, then
  K120 sts of first leg. (240 sts)
Starting with a P row, work 29 rows in st st, so
  ending with a P row.
Next row (RS) *K1, K2tog, rep from * to end.
  (160 sts)

K 3 rows.
Cast off.

TROUSER PATCH
With white, cast on 20 sts.
K 2 rows (garter st).
*Next row (WS) K2, P16, K2.
K one row.*
Rep from * to * 7 times more.
K 2 rows.
Cast off.

SLEEVE CUFFS (make 2)
With green, cast on 40 sts.
Starting with a K row, work 4 rows in st st, so ending with a P row.
Cast off loosely.

FINISHING
Trousers Join centre back seam (row ends) of trousers from top to point where legs were joined on. Then join each leg seam. Turn right side out.

Starting at centre back, work running st round waist in centre of garter st waistband, leaving long loose ends.

Put trousers on doll and pull each end to gather waist, knot and stitch to centre back body seam.

Trouser patch Using red, embroider two holly berries at centre of patch. Using green, embroider three holly leaves around berries.

With mid-blue, sew patch to a trouser leg at knee, working big untidy straight stitches (see detail on page 52).

Sleeve cuffs Join row ends of cuff, then turn right side out. Slip cuffs onto arms and position so that cast-off edge is level with fourth row of first green stripe on sleeve and cast-on edge overlaps hand. Sew each cuff in place along the cast-off edge.

HAT

TO MAKE
With white, cast on 120 sts.
K 11 rows (garter st).
Starting with a P row, work 9 rows in st st, so ending with a P row.
Break off white and change to red.
Next row (RS) K28, (K2tog) twice, K56, (K2tog) twice, K28. (116 sts)

P one row.
Next row K27, (K2tog) twice, K54, (K2tog) twice, K27. (112 sts)
P one row.
Next row K26, (K2tog) twice, K52, (K2tog) twice, K26. (108 sts)
P one row.
Continue in st st, decreasing 4 sts on every other row in this way until 8 sts remain.
Break off yarn leaving a long loose end.
Using a blunt-ended needle, thread loose end through all 8 sts on needle, pull yarn to gather tightly, then fasten off.

HOLLY LEAVES (make 2)
With green, cast on 20 sts.
K one row.
P one row.
Next row (picot row) (RS) *Yfwd, K2tog, rep from * to end. (20 sts)
P one row.
K one row.
Cast off purlwise.

BERRY
With red, cast on 20 sts.
K one row.
P one row.
Cast off.

FINISHING
With right sides tog, join hat seam (row ends), using matching yarn for each section. Turn right side out.

Turn up brim to RS and sew cast-on edge to last row of white. Stuff hat lightly and sew in place on top of head, stitching all round folded edge of brim.

Pompon With white, make a pompon (see instructions on pages 11-12) 5 cm (2 in) in diameter and sew to end of hat.

Bend the end of hat down to one side and sew in place.

Holly With wrong sides tog, fold one holly leaf in half along picot row and join cast-on edge to cast-off edge. Then fold joined edge tog and sew down centre of leaf (so that picot edge forms outer edge of leaf). Finish other leaf in same way. Sew bottom of each leaf to brim of hat in same place.

Roll up holly berry (strip) and sew a few stitches through berry to secure shape. Sew berry to base of leaves.

ANIMAL MAGIC

TEDDY BEARS' PICNIC

Greedy pig is certainly not one to miss out on the scrumptious lunch box that Ted and Teresa Bear, Panda and Baby Panda have brought along to their picnic.

MATERIALS FOR TED BEAR

- Double knitting yarn: 75 g beige for bear, 50 g yellow for sweater, 50 g dark green for trousers
- Small amounts of double knitting yarn in red for bag and black for features
- Pair of 3¼ mm (old size 10) knitting needles *or size to obtain correct tension*
- Good quality washable stuffing
- Snap fastener for sweater
- 40 cm (16 in) of 5 mm (¼ in) wide elastic for trousers

TED BEAR

SIZE Ted Bear measures approx 30.5 cm (12 in) in height, when worked in recommended tension

TENSION 27 sts and 38 rows to 10 cm (4 in) measured over st st and worked on 3¼ mm needles
Check your tension before beginning and change needle size if necessary.

BEAR

BODY AND HEAD
Work body and head as for Benge Bunny (see page 68), but use beige instead of white.

ARMS AND LEGS
Work as for Benge Bunny, but use beige instead of white.

EARS (make 2)
With beige, cast on 20 sts.
Starting with a K row, work 12 rows in st st, so ending with a P row.
Next row (RS) (K2tog) twice, K12, (K2tog) twice. (16 sts)
Starting with a P row, work 9 rows in st st.
Cast off.

FINISHING
Finish body and head, legs and arms as for Benge Bunny, but use beige yarn instead of white to shape the neck.
Ears Fold one ear in half with right sides tog. Join side seam (row ends) on first side of ear and when top of ear is reached, secure yarn but

do not break off. Now work a running st along fold, pull yarn to gather top of ear slightly and secure yarn, then continue seam down other side of ear joining row ends and leaving lower edge open. Turn ear right side out.

Oversew cast-on and cast-off edge tog. Sew other ear tog in the same way. Sew ears onto the head.

Embroidery Using black yarn and working in satin st, make a triangle (with one corner pointing downwards) for nose. Still using black, work a vertical straight st from tip of nose to centre of mouth, then work a V-shape on both sides of centre of mouth.

Using black, embroider eyes (see page 10).

SWEATER

BACK AND FRONT

The back and front of Ted Bear's sweater are worked in one piece, starting at the lower edge of the front as follows.

With yellow, cast on 40 sts.

1st rib row (RS) *K1, P1, rep from * to end.

Rep last row 3 times more.

Starting with a K row, work 24 rows in st st, so ending with a P row.

NECK SHAPING

Next row (RS) K10, turn leaving rem 30 sts on a st holder.

Working on first side of neck only, continue as follows:

Cast on 10 sts at end of last row. (20 sts)

**Next row K2, P to end.

Next row K to end.**

Rep from ** to ** 6 times more, so ending with a RS row. Break off yarn and slip these 20 sts onto a st holder.

Return to 30 sts on first st holder and with RS facing, rejoin yarn and cast off centre 20 sts, K to end of row. (10 sts)

Next row P to end.

Cast on 12 sts at end of last row. (22 sts)

***Next row K to end.

Next row P20, K2.***

Rep from *** to *** 5 times more, so ending with a WS row.

Next row Cast off 2 sts, K to end. (20 sts)

Next row P20, then with WS facing, P20 from st holder. (40 sts)

Starting with a K row, work 10 rows in st st, so ending with a P row.

Rep first rib row 4 times.
Cast off in rib.

SLEEVES (make 2)

With yellow, cast on 34 sts.

Rep first rib row of sweater 4 times.

Starting with a K row, work 18 rows in st st. Cast off.

FINISHING

Sew cast-off edge of sleeves to sides of sweater. Join sleeve and side seams. Sew 2-st cast-off edge at bottom of neck slit to inside of back. Sew snap fastener to top of neck slit.

TROUSERS

TO MAKE

The 2 legs are worked separately and then joined at the top.

FIRST LEG

*With dark green, cast on 40 sts.

K 4 rows (garter st).

Starting with a P row, work 25 rows in st st, so ending with a P row.*

Break off yarn and slip sts onto a spare needle. This completes first leg.

SECOND LEG

Rep from * to * for second leg. Do not break off yarn.

JOINING LEGS

With RS facing, K40 sts of second leg, then K40 sts of first leg from spare needle. (80 sts)

Starting with a P row, work 19 rows in st st, so ending with a P row.

Next row (RS) *Yfwd, K2tog, rep from * to end. (80 sts)

K one row. Cast off.

FINISHING

Join centre back seam (row ends) of trousers from top to point where legs were joined on. Then join each leg seam. Turn RS out. Thread elastic through eyelet holes and join ends.

BAG

MAIN PIECE

With red, cast on 14 sts.

Starting with a K row, work 32 rows in st st. Cast off.

STRAP
With red, cast on 40 sts.
K one row.
Cast off.

FINISHING
Fold bag along thirteenth row from cast-off

edge with right sides tog. Join side seams (row ends). Turn bag right side out.

Sew the ends of the strap to the sides of the top of the bag.

Fold flap over front of bag and stitch in place.

Using black yarn and working in satin st, embroider a 'button' at centre of flap.

★ ★

MATERIALS FOR TERESA BEAR

- Double knitting yarn:
  75 g beige for bear,
  50 g white for
  sweater, 50 g red for
  skirt
- Small amounts of
  double knitting yarn in
  dark pink for bag and
  black for features
- Pair of 3¼ mm (old
  size 10) knitting
  needles *or size to
  obtain correct tension*
- Good quality washable
  stuffing
- Snap fastener for
  sweater
- 40 cm (16 in) of 5 mm
  (¼ in) wide elastic for
  skirt

TERESA BEAR

SIZE As for Ted Bear

TENSION As for Ted Bear

BEAR

TO MAKE
Work bear, sweater and bag as for Ted Bear, but use white instead of yellow for sweater and dark pink instead of red for bag.
Then make skirt that follows, or alternatively, pinafore as for Betsey Bunny (see page 71).

SKIRT

TO MAKE

With red, cast on 100 sts.
K 4 rows (garter st).
Starting with a P row, work 23 rows in st st, so ending with a P row.
Next row (RS) *Yfwd, K2tog, rep from * to end. (100 sts)
K one row. Cast off.

FINISHING
Join centre back seam (row ends) of skirt and turn right side out. Thread elastic through

Right: *Teresa Bear*

MATERIALS FOR PANDAS

- Double knitting yarn: 75 g white for body, head and tail and 40 g black for ears, legs and arms
- Small amount of double knitting yarn in red for mouth
- Pair of 3¼ mm (old size 10) knitting needles *or size to obtain correct tension*
- Good quality washable stuffing
- Small pieces of black and white felt for eyes
- Red pencil for cheeks

PANDA AND BABY PANDA

SIZE Panda measures approx 15 cm (6 in) in height and Baby Panda measures approx 10 cm (4 in) in height (including ears), when worked in recommended tension

TENSION As for Ted Bear

TO MAKE
Work Panda as for Daddy and Mummy Bear and Baby Panda as for Baby Bear (see the instructions for The Three Bears on page 98), but use white instead of light brown for body and head and use black instead of brown for arms, legs and ears.

FINISHING
Finish body and head, arms, legs and ears as for Three Bears, but use white to shape the neck.
Embroidery Using a single 'ply' of red yarn, work a V-shaped mouth.

Using black yarn, work a short horizontal straight st and work once or twice over the same st for nose.

Eyes are worked in appliqué. Cut two pieces of black felt and two pieces of white felt in the shapes and sizes shown in the diagram. Then sew white inner eyes to black eyes in positions shown. Using a single 'ply' of black yarn, work a French knot on each white inner eye for pupils. Sew slanting eyes to head.

Colour cheeks with red pencil.

★ ★

MATERIALS FOR PIG

- Double knitting yarn: 40 g light pink for body, head and tail and 25 g dark pink for ears, legs, arms and nose
- Small amount of double knitting yarn in black for eyes
- Pair of 3¼ mm (old size 10) knitting needles *or size to obtain correct tension*
- Good quality washable stuffing
- Red pencil for cheeks

PIG

SIZE Pig measures approx 14 cm (5½ in) in height (including ears), when worked in recommended tension

TENSION As for Ted Bear

BODY AND HEAD
Work as for Daddy and Mummy Bear (see instructions on page 98), but use light pink instead of light brown.

ARMS AND LEGS
Work as for Daddy and Mummy Bear, but use dark pink instead of brown.

EARS (make 2)
With dark pink, cast on 14 sts.
Starting with a K row, work 8 rows in st st, so ending with a P row.
Next row (RS) (K2tog) 7 times. (7 sts)
P one row.
Next row K into front and back of each st. (14 sts)
Starting with a P row, work 8 rows in st st, so ending with a K row.
Cast off purlwise.

NOSE
With dark pink, cast on 7 sts.

1st row (RS) K into front and back of each st. (14 sts)
Starting with a P row, work 7 rows in st st.
Next row (RS) (K2tog) 7 times. (7 sts)
Cast off purlwise.

TAIL
With light pink, cast on 20 sts.
Starting with a K row, work 4 rows in st st.
Cast off.

FINISHING
Finish body and head and arms and legs as for Daddy and Mummy Bear (see page 98), but use light pink to shape neck.
Ears Fold ears in half along row between inc and dec rows, with wrong sides tog. Join side seams (row ends) and join cast-on and cast-off edges tog. Do not stuff.

Sew cast-on/cast-off edge of ears to the head, so that ears lie flat with their folded edge pointing outwards.
Tail With wrong sides tog, join cast-on edge to cast-off edge, pulling stitches tightly to curl tail. Sew tail to bottom centre back of Pig.
Nose Sew nose to front of head with cast-on and cast-off edges at top and bottom.
Embroidery Using light pink yarn, embroider French knots on top of nose for nostrils.

Using black yarn, embroider the eyes (see page 10). Colour cheeks with red pencil.

PANDA

Cut two from black felt

Cut two from white felt

BABY PANDA

Cut two from black felt

Cut two from white felt

MATERIALS FOR LUNCH BOX

- Small amounts of double knitting yarn in white, red, light brown, dark brown, orange, black, gold, green, yellow and blue
- Pair of 3¼ mm (old size 10) knitting needles *or size to obtain correct tension*
- Good quality washable stuffing
- Piece of plastic (see Finishing)

Above: *Pig, Panda and Baby Panda*

LUNCH BOX FEAST

SIZE Bakewell Tart, Mince Pie, Apple and Orange each measure approx 6 cm (2¼ in) in diameter, Pasty measures approx 10 cm (4 in) in length, Bottle of Limeade measures approx 12 cm (4¾ in) in height, and Choc Bar measures approx 8 cm (3 in) in length, when worked in recommended tension

TENSION 27 sts and 38 rows to 10 cm (4 in) measured over st st and worked on 3¼ mm needles
Check your tension before beginning and change needle size if necessary.

BAKEWELL TART

PASTRY CASE
With light brown, cast on 40 sts.
Starting with a K row, work 4 rows in st st, so ending with a P row.
Next row (picot row) (RS) *Yfwd, K2tog, rep from * to end. (40 sts)
Starting with a P row, work 4 rows more in st st, so ending with a K row.
K one row.
**Next row (RS) *K3, K2tog, rep from * to end. (32 sts)
P one row.

Next row *K2, K2tog, rep from * to end. (24 sts)
P one row.
Next row *K1, K2tog, rep from * to end. (16 sts)
P one row.
Next row (K2tog) 8 times. (8 sts)
Break off yarn leaving a long loose end.
Using a blunt-ended needle, thread loose end through all 8 sts on needle, pull yarn to gather tightly, then fasten off.**

ICING
With white, cast on 40 sts.
K one row.
P one row.
Complete as for Pastry Case from ** to **.

CHERRY
With red, cast on 3 sts.
1st row (RS) K into front and back of each st. (6 sts)
Starting with a P row, work 3 rows in st st, so ending with a P row.
Next row (RS) (K2tog) 3 times. (3 sts)
Break off yarn leaving a long loose end and fasten off as for Pastry Case.

FINISHING
Join row ends of pastry case. Turn first four rows of pastry case to WS along picot row to form sides of pastry case and stitch in place.

Bakewell tart

Mince pie

Orange

Apple

Using a soft plastic ice cream container, cut a circle 4.5 cm (1¾ in) in diameter and place inside the bottom of the pastry case.

Join row ends of icing. Put a little stuffing inside pastry case over plastic circle, then sew icing to sides of pastry case.

Join row ends of cherry with wrong sides tog and sew cast-on and cast-off edges tog. Sew cherry to top of tart.

MINCE PIE

TO MAKE

Make Pastry Case as for Bakewell Tart. Then make Icing as for Bakewell Tart, but using light brown instead of white.

Finish as for Bakewell Tart, omitting cherry. Using dark brown yarn, work 3 straight stitches on top of pie to represent holes.

ORANGE

TO MAKE

With orange, cast on 9 sts.

1st row K into front and back of each st. (18 sts)
P one row.

Next row K into front and back of each st. (36 sts)

Starting with a P row, work 15 rows in st st, so ending with a P row.

Next row (K2tog) 18 times. (18 sts)
P one row.

Next row (K2tog) 9 times. (9 sts)
P one row. 3

Break off yarn leaving a long loose end and fasten off as for Pastry Case.

FINISHING

With K sides tog, join row ends of Orange, leaving cast-on end open. Turn right side out (P side on outside).

Stuff firmly. Oversew cast-on edge every alternate st, pull yarn to gather tightly and fasten off. Using black yarn, embroider a 'star' at centre top of Orange to represent a stalk.

APPLE

TO MAKE

Work as for Orange, but using red yarn instead of orange yarn.

LEAVES (make 2)

With green, cast on 4 sts.
K 2 rows.
Cast off.

FINISHING

With P sides tog, join row ends of Apple, leaving cast-on end open. Turn right side out (K side on outside). Stuff firmly.

To shape Apple, secure a length of red yarn to centre top and pass needle from centre top to centre bottom, then back up to top. Pull yarn a little to make indents at top and bottom, then fasten off yarn.

Stalk Take an 18 cm (7 in) length of dark brown yarn, and fold in three, then in half again. Wind dark brown yarn tightly round the loops, sewing a couple of stitches at top and bottom to secure. Sew stalk to top of Apple.

Sew leaves in place at base of stalk.

PASTY

TO MAKE

With gold, cast on 64 sts.

1st rib row (RS) *K1, P1, rep from * to end.
Rep last row 3 times more.

Next row (RS) *K6, K2tog, rep from * to end. (56 sts)
P one row.

Next row *K5, K2tog, rep from * to end. (48 sts)
P one row.

Next row *K4, K2tog, rep from * to end. (40 sts)
P one row.

Complete Pasty as for Pastry Case of Bakewell Tart from ** to ** (see instructions given on page 61).

FINISHING

Join row ends of Pasty. Fold Pasty in half with wrong sides tog, then stitch through top and bottom of pasty along last rib row, leaving a gap for stuffing.

Stuff firmly and finish sewing along the last rib row.

Join the cast-on edge of top and bottom of Pasty together.

Using dark brown yarn, work 3 straight stitches on top of Pasty to represent air holes (see photograph).

CHOC BAR

CHOCOLATE

With dark brown, cast on 13 sts.
1st row (WS) Knit.
2nd row (RS) *P1, K3, rep from * to last st, P1.
3rd row *K1, P3, rep from * to last st, K1.
4th row As 2nd row.
Rep 1st-4th rows 4 times more.
Starting with a K (WS) row, work 20 rows in
  st st.
Cast off.

WRAPPER

With white, cast on 30 sts.
K one row.
P one row.
Break off white and change to red.
K 3 rows (garter st).
Starting with a P row, work 11 rows in st st,
  so ending with a P row.
Break off red and change to white.
K one row.
P one row.

WRAPPER FLAP SHAPING

Next row K6, turn leaving rem 24 sts on a st
  holder.
Working on these 6 sts only and starting with a
  P row, work 3 rows in st st.
Cast off.
**Return to rem sts on st holder and with RS
  facing and using white, K6 sts from st holder,
  then starting with a P row, work 3 rows in st st
  on these 6 sts only and cast off.**
Rep from ** to ** 3 times more.

FINISHING

Chocolate With right sides tog, join cast-on
and cast-off edges of chocolate and join row
ends at one side. Turn right side out.
  Using a soft plastic ice cream container, cut a
piece of plastic 4.5 cm (1¾ in) by 6.5 cm
(2½ in) and slip inside chocolate. Oversew the
remaining side.
Wrapper With wrong sides tog, join row ends
of wrapper. Then with seam at centre back, join
cast-on edge.
  Slip chocolate into wrapper. Fold flaps down
and sew five flaps to RS of wrapper (stitching
through chocolate) so that it looks as if the
chocolate is unwrapped at top.
  Using black yarn, embroider 'CHOC BAR' on
front of wrapper.

BOTTLE OF LIMEADE

BOTTLE

With green, cast on 20 sts.
Starting with a K row, work 12 rows in st st,
  so ending with a P row.
Next row (RS) *K1, K into front and back of next
  st, rep from * to end. (30 sts)
Starting with a P row, work 5 rows in st st,
  so ending with a P row.
Next row (RS) *K2, K into front and back of next
  st, rep from * to end. (40 sts)
Starting with a P row, work 20 rows in st st,
  so ending with a K row.
K one row.
Complete as for Pastry Case of Bakewell Tart
  from ** to **.

LABEL

With white, cast on 30 sts.
Starting with a K row, work 12 rows in st st, so
  ending with a P row.
Cast off.

BOTTLE TOP

With yellow, cast on 30 sts.
K 2 rows (garter st).
P one row.
Next row (RS) *K3, K2tog, rep from * to end.
  (24 sts)
Next row *P2, P2tog, rep from * to end.
  (18 sts)
Next row (K2tog) 9 times. (9 sts)
Break off yarn leaving a long loose end.
Using a blunt-ended needle, thread loose end
  through all 9 sts on needle, pull yarn to gather
  tightly, then fasten off.

FINISHING

Join row ends of bottle up to 2.5 cm (1 in) from
top. Turn right side out.
  Using a soft plastic ice cream container, cut a
circle of plastic 4.5 cm (1¾ in) in diameter (same
size as bottom of bottle) and slip this plastic
piece in place inside base of bottle.
  Finish joining row ends and stuff bottle lightly.
  Join row ends of bottle top and sew to top of
the bottle.
  Sew label on bottle.
  Using a single 'ply' of black yarn, embroider
'LIMEADE' onto label.
  Using blue yarn, work a running st 5 mm (¼ in)
from edge all round edge of label.

Pasty

Choc bar

Limeade

THE MOUSE FAMILY

Home Sweet Home is a cosy cottage for this charming family of mice. Small enough to fit into most dolls' houses, Mr Mouse, Mrs Mouse and Baby Mouse will delight any young child and stimulate hours of imaginative play.

MATERIALS FOR MOUSE FAMILY
· Double knitting yarn: 30 g light brown for heads, feet, hands and tail, 25 g lilac for dress
· Small amounts of double knitting yarn in red for mouths, red and white for Baby Mouse's body, green and yellow for Mr Mouse, mid-blue for bow, black for eyes, dark pink for noses
· Pair of 3¼ mm (old size 10) knitting needles *or size to obtain correct tension*
· Good quality washable stuffing

SIZE Mr and Mrs Mouse measure approx 11 cm (4¼ in) in height and Baby Mouse measures approx 7.5 cm (3 in) in height (including ears), when worked in recommended tension

TENSION 27 sts and 38 rows to 10 cm (4 in) measured over st st and worked on 3¼ mm needles
Check your tension before beginning and change needle size if necessary.

MR MOUSE
BODY AND HEAD
With green, cast on 19 sts.
1st row (RS) K into front and back of each st. (38 sts)
Starting with a P row, work 9 rows in st st, so ending with a P row.
P one row.
Break off green and change to yellow.
Starting with a P row, work 6 rows more in st st, so ending with a K row.
NECK SHAPING
Next row (WS) (P2tog) 19 times. (19 sts)
Break off yellow and change to light brown for head.
Next row *K1, K into front and back of next st, rep from * to last st, K1. (28 sts)
HEAD SHAPING
****Next row** P13, (P into front and back of next st) twice, P13. (30 sts)
Next row K14, (K into front and back of next st) twice, K14. (32 sts)
****Next row** P to centre 2 sts, P into front and back of each of 2 centre sts, P to end.
Next row K to centre 2 sts, K into front and back of each of 2 centre sts, K to end.**
Rep from ** to ** once more. (40 sts)
Next row P18, (P2tog) twice, P18. (38 sts)

Next row K17, (K2tog) twice, K17. (36 sts)
****Next row** P to 4 centre sts, (P2tog) twice, P to end.
Next row K to centre 4 sts, (K2tog) twice, K to end.***
Rep from *** to *** once more. (28 sts)
Next row (P2tog) 14 times. (14 sts)
Next row (K2tog) 7 times. (7 sts)
Break off yarn leaving a long loose end.
Using a blunt-ended needle, thread loose end through all 7 sts on needle, pull yarn to gather tightly, then fasten off.

ARMS (make 2)
With yellow, cast on 10 sts.
Starting with a K row, work 7 rows in st st, so ending with a K row.
K one row.
Break off yellow and change to light brown for hand.
Starting with a K row, work 4 rows in st st, so ending with a P row.
Next row (RS) (K2tog) 5 times. (5 sts)
Break off yarn leaving a long loose end and fasten off as for body and head.

FEET (make 2)
With light brown, cast on 10 sts.
Starting with a K row, work 8 rows in st st, so ending with a P row.
Next row (RS) (K2tog) 5 times. (5 sts)
Break off yarn leaving a long loose end and fasten off as for body and head.

EARS (make 2)
With light brown, cast on 10 sts.
Starting with a K row, work 4 rows in st st, so ending with a P row.
Next row (RS) (K2tog) 5 times. (5 sts)
Break off yarn leaving a long loose end and fasten off as for body and head.

TAIL

With light brown, cast on 6 sts.
Starting with a K row, work 36 rows in st st, so ending with a P row.
Next row (RS) (K2tog) 3 times. (3 sts)
Break off yarn leaving a long loose end and fasten off as for body and head.

FINISHING

Body and head Join centre back seam (row ends) of body and head, using matching yarn for each section and leaving lower edge of body open. Turn right side out.

Stuff body and head firmly. Oversew cast-on edge every alternate st, pull yarn to gather tightly and fasten off.

To shape neck wrap a length of yellow yarn twice round the neck between the dec and inc rows. Pull yarn tightly to gather neck, knot at centre back neck and sew ends into neck.

Arms and feet Join leg and arm seams (row ends) with wrong sides tog and oversew cast-on edges tog, keeping seams at centre . Do not stuff. Sew feet to bottom of body with seams facing downwards. Sew one arm to each side of body just below neck with seams facing body.

Ears Join each ear seam (row ends) with wrong sides tog and oversew cast-on edges tog, keeping seam at side.

Sew ears to top of head.

Tail Fold tail in half lengthways with wrong sides tog. Join tail seam (row ends), pulling sts tightly while stitching to curl tail. Sew tail to centre bottom back of mouse.

Embroidery Using a single 'ply' of dark pink yarn and working in satin st, work a round nose at end of point on head.

Using a single 'ply' of red, work a horizontal straight st for mouth. Using black yarn, embroider eyes (see page 10).

MRS MOUSE

BODY AND HEAD

With light brown, cast on 14 sts.
1st row (WS) K into front and back of each st. (28 sts)
Starting with a P row, work 16 rows in st st, so ending with a K row.

NECK SHAPING
Next row (WS) (P2tog) 14 times. (14 sts)
Next row K into front and back of each st. (28 sts)

Complete head as for Mr Mouse from ****.

ARMS AND LEGS

Work as for Mr Mouse, but use lilac for yellow on arms.

EARS AND TAIL

Work as for Mr Mouse.

DRESS

With lilac, cast on 30 sts.
Starting with a K row, work 5 rows in st st, so ending with a K row.
Next row (WS) *P1, P into front and back of next st, rep from * to end. (45 sts)
Starting with a K row, work 13 rows in st st, so ending with a K row.
K one row.
Cast off.

FINISHING

Begin finishing as for Mr Mouse, but before sewing on arms put dress on mouse and join centre back seam (row ends). Sew on arms as for Mr Mouse, but stitching through dress.

Complete finishing as for Mr Mouse. Then starting at centre front and using mid-blue yarn, work a row of running st through inc row of dress and tie ends in a bow at centre front for a decorative belt along waistline.

Below: Mrs Mouse

BABY MOUSE

BODY AND HEAD

With red, cast on 13 sts.

1st row (RS) K into front and back of each st.
  (26 sts)

Starting with a P row, work 5 rows in st st,
  so ending with a P row.

P one row.

Break off red and change to white.

Starting with a P row, work 4 rows more in st st,
  so ending with a K row.

NECK SHAPING

Next row (WS) (P2tog) 13 times. (13 sts)

Break off white and change to light brown.

Next row *K1, K into front and back of next st,
  rep from * to last st, K into front and back of
  last st. (20 sts)

HEAD SHAPING

Next row P9, (P into front and back of next st)
  twice, P9. (22 sts)

Next row K10, (K into front and back of next st)
  twice, K10. (24 sts)

Next row P11, P into front and back of each of
  2 centre sts, P11. (26 sts)

Next row K12, K into front and back of each of
  2 centre sts, K12. (28 sts)

Next row P12, (P2tog) twice, P12. (26 sts)

Next row K11, (K2tog) twice, K11. (24 sts)

Next row P10, (P2tog) twice, P10. (22 sts)

Next row K9, (K2tog) twice, K9. (20 sts)

Next row (P2tog) 10 times. (10 sts)

Next row (K2tog) 5 times. (5 sts)

Break off yarn leaving a long loose end.

Using a blunt-ended needle, thread loose end
  through all 5 sts on needle, pull yarn to gather
  tightly, then fasten off.

ARMS (make 2)

With white, cast on 6 sts.

Starting with a K row, work 5 rows in st st,
  so ending with a K row.

K one row.

Break off white and change to light brown for
  hand.

Starting with a K row, work 2 rows in st st,
  so ending with a P row.

Next row (RS) (K2tog) 3 times. (3 sts)

Break off yarn leaving a long loose end and
  fasten off as for body and head.

FEET (make 2)

With light brown, cast on 6 sts.

Starting with a K row, work 6 rows in st st,
  so ending with a P row.

Next row (RS) (K2tog) 3 times. (3 sts)

Break off yarn leaving a long loose end and
  fasten off as for body and head.

EARS (make 2)

With light brown, cast on 6 sts.

Starting with a K row, work 3 rows in st st,
  so ending with a K row.

Next row (WS) (P2tog) 3 times. (3 sts)

Break off yarn leaving a long loose end and
  fasten off as for body and head.

TAIL

With light brown, cast on 4 sts.

Starting with a K row, work 24 rows in st st,
  so ending with a P row.

Next row (RS) (K2tog) twice. (2 sts)

Next row P2tog.

Fasten off.

FINISHING

Sew Baby Mouse together as for Mr Mouse.

Embroidery Using a single 'ply' of dark pink
yarn and working in satin st, work a round nose
at end of point on head.

  Using a single 'ply' of red, work a horizontal
straight st for mouth. Using black yarn, make
the eyes (see instructions on page 10).

Above: *Mr Mouse and Baby Mouse*

BENGE AND BETSEY BUNNY

Benge and Betsey Bunny are cheeky little rabbits with keen appetites and a discerning eye for choice vegetables in the kitchen garden. To guard against hunger, they always keep a spare carrot tucked in their pocket, ready to nibble.

MATERIALS FOR BENGE BUNNY

- Double knitting yarn: 50 g white for body, 40 g blue for dungarees, 20 g pink for ears
- Small amounts of double knitting yarn in black, red, green and orange for features and carrot
- Pair of 3¼ mm (old size 10) knitting needles *or size to obtain correct tension*
- Good quality washable stuffing
- Red and black pencils for cheeks and lines on carrot

BENGE BUNNY

SIZE Benge measures approx 37 cm (14½ in) in height (including ears), when worked in recommended tension

TENSION 27 sts and 38 rows to 10 cm (4 in) measured over st st and worked on 3¼ mm needles
Check your tension before beginning and change needle size if necessary.

BUNNY

BODY AND HEAD
With white, cast on 60 sts.
Starting with a K row, work 32 rows in st st, so ending with a P row.
NECK SHAPING
Next row (RS) (K2tog) 30 times. (30 sts)
P one row.
Next row K into front and back of each st. (60 sts)
Starting with a P row, work 29 rows more in st st for head, so ending with a P row.
Next row (RS) (K2tog) 30 times. (30 sts)
Next row (P2tog) 15 times. (15 sts)
Break off yarn leaving a long loose end.
Using a blunt-ended needle, thread loose end through all 15 sts on needle, pull yarn to gather tightly, then fasten off.

ARMS (make 2)
With white, cast on 13 sts.
1st row (RS) K into front and back of each st. (26 sts)
Starting with a P row, work 35 rows in st st, so ending with a P row.
Next row (RS) (K2tog) 13 times. (13 sts)
Break off yarn leaving a long loose end. Using a

blunt-ended needle, thread loose end through all 13 sts on needle, pull yarn to gather tightly, then fasten off.

LEGS (make 2)
With white, cast on 24 sts.
1st row (RS) K into front and back of each st. (48 sts)
Starting with a P row, work 13 rows in st st, so ending with a P row.
Next row (RS) K10, (K3tog) 9 times, K11. (30 sts)
Starting with a P row, work 27 rows more in st st. Cast off.

EARS (make 2)
With white, cast on 20 sts.
Starting with a K row, work 30 rows in st st, so ending with a P row.
Next row (RS) (K2tog) twice, K12, (K2tog) twice. (16 sts)
P one row.
Break off white and change to pink.
With pink and starting with a K row, work 28 rows in st st.
Cast off.

FINISHING

Body and head Join centre back seam (row ends) of body and head, leaving lower edge of body open. Turn right side out.
  Stuff body and head firmly. Then oversew lower edge of body tog, keeping seam at centre back.
  To shape neck wrap a length of white yarn twice round the neck between the dec and inc rows. Pull yarn tightly to gather neck, knot at centre back neck and sew ends into neck.
Legs Join lower edge and centre back seam (row ends) of each leg, leaving top edge of each leg open. Turn legs right side out.

Stuff each leg firmly and oversew top edge tog, keeping seam at centre back. Sew legs to lower edge of body.

Arms Join arm seams (row ends), leaving top of each arm open. Turn arms right side out.

Stuff each arm firmly and oversew top edge tog, keeping seam at centre.

Sew one arm to each side of body, joining top of each arm horizontally to body about two rows below neck shaping.

Ears Fold one ear in half with RS of pink half facing RS of white half. Join side seam (row ends) on first side of ear and when top of ear is reached, secure yarn but do not break off. Now work a running st through top of ear one row from where pink begins, pull yarn to gather top of ear slightly and secure yarn, then continue seam down other side of ear joining row ends and leaving lower edge open. Do not break off yarn. Turn ear right side out.

Secure yarn, then with WS of white side of ear facing wrong side of pink side of ear, work a running st through both layers along lower edge, pull yarn to gather bottom of ear tightly and fasten off yarn.

Sew other ear tog in same way.

Sew ears to top of head, with pink sides facing front.

Embroidery Using a single 'ply' of red yarn and working in satin st, make a triangle (with one corner pointing downwards) for nose. Then still using red, work a vertical straight st about 1.5 cm (½ in) long from centre of tip of nose to centre of mouth. Work a straight st from centre of mouth slanting slightly upwards to the right, then work the other half of the mouth to the left in the same way.

Using black yarn, embroider eyes (see instructions on page 10).

Colour cheeks with red pencil (see page 11 for how to colour cheeks).

DUNGAREES

TO MAKE
The 2 legs are worked separately and then joined at the top.

FIRST LEG
*With blue, cast on 40 sts.
K 4 rows (garter st).
Starting with a P row, work 25 rows in st st, so ending with a P row.*

Break off yarn and slip sts onto a spare needle. This completes first leg.

SECOND LEG
Rep from * to * for second leg. Do not break off yarn.

JOINING LEGS
With RS facing, K40 sts of second leg, then K40 sts of first leg. (80 sts)
Starting with a P row, work 16 rows in st st, so ending with a RS row.
Next row (WS) K31, P18, K31.**
K one row.
Rep from ** to ** once.

BIB SHAPING
Next row (RS) Cast off 29 sts, K22 (counting st already on needle after cast off), cast off rem 29 sts. (22 sts)
Next row With WS facing, rejoin yarn, then K2, P18, K2.
K one row.
***Next row K2, P18, K2.
K one row.***
Rep from *** to *** 6 times more.
K 3 rows.
Cast off.

POCKET
With blue, cast on 15 sts.
Starting with a K row, work 13 rows in st st, so ending with a K row.
K one row.
Cast off.

STRAPS (make 2)
With blue, cast on 40 sts.
K 4 rows. Cast off.

FINISHING
Join centre back seam (row ends) of dungarees from top to point where legs were joined on. Then join each leg seam. Turn right side out.

Sew pocket to bib, placing pocket so that top (garter st edge) is 1.5 cm (½ in) below cast-off edge of bib.

Put dungarees on bunny and sew one end of each strap to corner of bib. Take straps over shoulders and cross at back of bunny, then sew other end of each strap to dungarees at waist 1.5 cm (½ in) from centre back seam, tucking any excess strap inside dungarees.

Tail With white, make a pompon (see pages 11-12) 4 cm (1½ in) in diameter and sew to back of dungarees below waist for tail.

Detail of carrots

MATERIALS FOR BETSEY BUNNY

- Double knitting yarn: 50 g white for body, 40 g yellow for pinafore, 20 g pink for ears
- Small amounts of double knitting yarn in black, red, green and orange for features and carrot
- Pair of 3¼ mm (old size 10) knitting needles *or size to obtain correct tension*
- Good quality washable stuffing
- Red and black pencils for cheeks and lines on carrot

CARROT

TO MAKE
With orange, cast on 16 sts.
K one row.
P one row.
*Next row (RS) K2tog, K to last 2 sts, K2tog.
P one row.*
Rep from * to * 5 times more. (4 sts rem)
Next row (RS) (K2tog) twice. (2 sts)
Next row P2tog. Fasten off.

CARROT TOP (make 2)
With green, cast on 20 sts. Cast off.

BETSEY BUNNY

SIZE As for Benge Bunny

TENSION As for Benge Bunny

BUNNY

TO MAKE
Make bunny and finish as for Benge Bunny.

PINAFORE

TO MAKE
With yellow, cast on 120 sts.
K 4 rows (garter st).
Starting with a P row, work 21 rows in st st, so ending with a P row.
Next row (RS) *K1, K2tog, rep from * to end. (80 sts)
Next row K31, P18, K31.
K one row. Rep from ** to ** once.
Bib shaping
Next row (RS) Cast off 29 sts, K22 (counting st already on needle after cast off), cast off rem 29 sts. (22 sts)
Next row With WS facing, rejoin yarn, then K2, P18, K2.
K one row.
***Next row K2, P18, K2.
K one row.***
Rep from *** to *** 6 times more.
K 3 rows. Cast off.

FINISHING
Join row ends of carrot, leaving top open and turn right side out.

Stuff carrot firmly, using tweezers. Work a running st along top edge of carrot for gathering, but do not break off yarn.

Hold green carrot tops tog and fold in half. Insert fold of green tops into top of carrot, pull yarn to gather carrot top and catch top with a few stitches to secure green tops firmly in place and close tops.

Draw a few short horizontal lines on carrot with black pencil for added detail.

Slip carrot into pocket of dungarees.

POCKET
With yellow, cast on 15 sts.
Starting with a K row, work 13 rows in st st, so ending with a K row.
K one row.
Cast off.

STRAPS (make 2)
With yellow, cast on 40 sts.
K 4 rows.
Cast off.

FINISHING
Join centre back seam (row ends) of pinafore skirt. Turn right side out.

Sew pocket to skirt, placing pocket so that top (garter st edge) is 1.5 cm (½ in) below skirt waistline.

Put pinafore on bunny and sew one end of each strap to corner of bib. Take straps over shoulders and cross at back of bunny, then sew other end of each strap to skirt at waist 1.5 cm (½ in) from centre back seam, tucking any excess strap inside skirt.

Tail With white, make a pompon (see instructions on pages 11-12 for how to make a pompom) 4 cm (1½ in) in diameter and sew to centre back of skirt below waist for tail.

CARROT

TO MAKE
Make and finish as for Benge Bunny and slip into pinafore pocket.

LITTLE FEATHERED FRIENDS

'Birds of a feather all flock together.' These four little feathered friends – the miniature Blue Bird, Robin and Duckling, plus the slightly bigger, wise old Owl – all look different but are inseparable companions nonetheless.

MATERIALS FOR BLUE BIRD, DUCKLING AND ROBIN

· Double knitting yarn: 25 g brown for Robin, 25 g white for Duckling, 25 g light blue for Blue Bird
· Small amounts of double knitting yarn in black for features and Robin's feet, light yellow for beaks, red for Robin and bright yellow for Duckling's feet
· Pair of 3¼ mm (old size 10) knitting needles *or size to obtain correct tension*
· Good quality washable stuffing

BIRDS

SIZE Blue Bird, Duck and Robin each measure approx 9 cm (3½ in) in height, when worked in recommended tension

TENSION 27 sts and 38 rows to 10 cm (4 in) measured over st st and worked on 3¼ mm needles
  Check your tension before beginning and change needle size if necessary.

BLUE BIRD

BODY AND HEAD
With light blue, cast on 16 sts.
1st row (RS) K into front and back of each st. (32 sts)
Starting with a P row, work 15 rows in st st, so ending with a P row. This completes body.
NECK SHAPING
***Next row** (RS) (K2tog) 16 times. (16 sts)
P one row.
Next row K into front and back of each st. (32 sts)
Starting with a P row, work 13 rows more in st st, so ending with a P row.
Next row (RS) (K2tog) 16 times. (16 sts)
Next row (P2tog) 8 times. (8 sts)
Break off yarn leaving a long loose end.
Using a blunt-ended needle, thread loose end through all 8 sts on needle, pull yarn to gather tightly, then fasten off.

WINGS (make 2)
With light blue, cast on 4 sts.
1st row (RS) K into front and back of each st. (8 sts)
Starting with a P row, work 9 rows in st st, so ending with a P row.

Next row (RS) K2tog, (yfwd, K2tog) 3 times. (7 sts)
Starting with a P row, work 9 rows in st st, so ending with a P row.
Next row (RS) (K2tog) 3 times, K1. (4 sts)
Cast off purlwise.

FEET (make 2)
With brown, cast on 3 sts.
1st row (RS) K into front and back of each st. (6 sts)
Starting with a P row, work 5 rows in st st, so ending with a P row.
Next row (RS) K2tog, (yfwd, K2tog) twice. (5 sts)
Starting with a P row, work 6 rows in st st, so ending with a K row. Cast off purlwise.

BEAK
With light yellow, cast on 6 sts.
Starting with a K row, work 6 rows in st st, so ending with a P row.
Next row (RS) (K2tog) 3 times. (3 sts)
P one row.
Next row K into front and back of each st. (6 sts)
Starting with a P row, work 6 rows in st st, so ending with a K row. Cast off purlwise.

TAIL
With light blue, cast on 6 sts.
1st row (RS) K into front and back of each st. (12 sts)
Starting with a P row, work 9 rows in st st, so ending with a P row.
TAIL SHAPING
Next row (RS) K4, turn leaving rem 8 sts unworked.
Next row P4.
Rep last 2 rows 3 times more. Break off yarn.
Next row (RS) Slip first 4 sts onto a st holder,

Above: *Blue Bird,
Duckling and Robin*

rejoin yarn to rem sts and K4, turn leaving
rem 4 sts on needle unworked.
Next row P4.
Next row K4, turn leaving rem 4 sts unworked.
Next row P4.
Rep last 2 rows 4 times.
Next row (RS) Slip first 4 sts onto a st holder,
  rejoin yarn to rem sts and K4.
Starting with a P row, work 7 rows more.
Break off yarn and with RS facing, slip middle
  4 sts and then first 4 sts back onto needle.
Next row With RS facing, K all 12 sts.
Starting with a P row, work 8 rows in st st, so
  ending with a K row.
Next row (WS) (P2tog) 6 times. (6 sts)
Cast off.

FINISHING
Body and head Join centre back (row ends) of
body and head, leaving lower edge of body
open. Turn right side out.
  Stuff body and head firmly. Oversew cast-on
edge every alternate st, pull yarn to gather
tightly and fasten off.
  To shape neck wrap a length of matching yarn
twice round the neck between the dec and inc
rows. Pull yarn tightly to gather neck, knot at
centre back neck and sew ends into neck.
Wings and feet Fold wings and feet in half
along holes with wrong sides tog. Join side
seams (row ends) and oversew cast-on and
cast-off edges tog, keeping seams at sides. Sew
feet to bottom of body with uneven edge facing
forwards. Sew one wing to each side of body
with the uneven edge facing backwards.
Tail Join seams on tail as for wing, then join

edges between three points gathering tips into
V-shapes as seam is worked.
Beak Join seam (row ends) of beak and sew to
front of head. (Do not stuff beak.)
Embroidery Using black yarn, embroider eyes
(see page 10).

ROBIN

BODY AND HEAD
With brown, cast on 16 sts.
1st row (RS) K into front and back of each st.
  (32 sts)
P one row.
Next row With brown K12, with red K8, with a
  separate length of brown K12.
Working centre 8 sts in red and twisting yarn
  when changing colours to avoid holes, start
  with a P row and work 13 rows in st st, so
  ending with a P row.
Break off red and continue in brown for head.
Work neck and head as for Blue Bird from ***.

WINGS AND TAIL
Work wings and tail in brown as for Blue Bird.

FEET
Work feet in black as for Blue Bird.

BEAK
With light yellow, cast on 8 sts.
K one row.
P one row.
Next row K2tog, K4, K2tog. (6 sts)
P one row.
Next row K2tog, K2, K2tog. (4 sts)
P one row.
Next row (K2tog) twice. (2 sts)
Next row P2tog. Fasten off.

FINISHING
Finish as for Blue Bird, but stuff beak lightly
before sewing to head.

DUCKLING

TO MAKE
Work as for Blue Bird, but use white for the
  wings, tail, body and head, and bright yellow
  for the feet. Stuff the beak lightly before
  sewing to the front of the head.

MATERIALS FOR OWL

- Double knitting yarn: 50 g brown for body and head, ears and wings, 25 g beige for chest
- Small amounts of double knitting yarn in black, mid-blue and white for features and in light yellow for feet and beak
- Pair of 3¼ mm (old size 10) knitting needles *or size to obtain correct tension*
- Good quality washable stuffing

OWL

SIZE Owl measures approx 14 cm (5½ in) in height, when worked in recommended tension

TENSION As for Blue Bird

BODY AND HEAD
Owl's body is worked in brown; the beige chest is worked separately and sewn on later.
With brown, cast on 25 sts.
1st row (RS) K into front and back of each st. (50 sts)
Starting with a P row, work 23 rows in st st.
NECK SHAPING
Next row (RS) (K2tog) 25 times. (25 sts)
P one row.
Next row K into front and back of each st. (50 sts)
Starting with a P row, work 21 rows more in st st for head, so ending with a P row.
Next row (RS) (K2tog) 25 times. (25 sts)
Next row (P2tog) 12 times, P1. (13 sts)
Break off yarn leaving a long loose end.
Using a blunt-ended needle, thread loose end through all 13 sts on needle, pull yarn to gather tightly, then fasten off.

CHEST
With beige, cast on 13 sts.
1st row (RS) K into front and back of each st. (26 sts)
Starting with a P row, work 23 rows in st st.
Next row (RS) (K2tog) 13 times. (13 sts)
Cast off purlwise.

WINGS (make 2)
With brown, cast on 16 sts.
1st row (RS) K into front and back of each st. (32 sts)
Starting with a P row, work 8 rows in st st.
Next row (WS) Cast off 3 sts, P to end. (29 sts)
Next row Cast off 3 sts, K to end. (26 sts)
Starting with a P row, work 4 rows in st st.
Next row (WS) Cast off 3 sts, P to end. (23 sts)
Next row Cast off 3 sts, K to end. (20 sts)
Starting with a P row, work 4 rows in st st.
Next row (WS) Cast off 3 sts, P to end. (17 sts)
Next row Cast off 3 sts, K to end. (14 sts)
Starting with a P row, work 3 rows in st st.
Next row (RS) (K2tog) 7 times. (7 sts)
Break off yarn leaving a long loose end and fasten off as for body and head.

FEET (make 2)
With light yellow, cast on 10 sts.
Starting with a K row, work 10 rows in st st.
Next row (RS) K1, (yfwd, K2tog) 4 times, K1. (10 sts)
Starting with a P row, work 10 rows in st st, so ending with a K row. Cast off purlwise.

EARS (make 2)
With brown, cast on 12 sts.
Starting with a K row, work 12 rows in st st. Cast off.

BEAK
With light yellow, cast on 12 sts.
K one row. P one row.
****Next row** K2tog, K to last 2 sts, K2tog.
P one row.**.
Rep from ** to ** 3 times more. (4 sts)
Next row (K2tog) twice. (2 sts)
Next row P2tog. Fasten off.

EYES (make 2)
With white, cast on 20 sts.
K one row. P one row.
Next row (K2tog) 10 times. (10 sts)
Break off yarn leaving a long loose end and fasten off as for body and head.

INNER EYES (make 2)
With mid-blue, cast on 10 sts.
1st row (K2tog) 5 times. (5 sts)
Break off yarn leaving a long loose end and fasten off as for body and head.

FINISHING
Body and head Finish as for Blue Bird, then sew chest piece to front of body with cast-on edge on neckline.
Wings Fold each wing in half lengthways, with wrong sides tog. Join row ends. Do not stuff. Sew cast-on edge of each wing to neckline.
Feet Follow instructions for Blue Bird and sew straight edge of feet to bottom of body.
Ears Fold ears in half diagonally with wrong sides tog. Sew sides tog. Sew diagonal folds of ears to top of head, with points facing forwards.
Eyes Join row ends of eyes. Sew eyes to head so that they are touching. Sew inner eyes to bottom of eyes. With black, work a French knot at centre of each inner eye to form pupils.
Beak With wrong sides tog, join row ends of beak, stuff lightly and sew to head.

GARDEN PARTY

★ ★

Big Tortoise has lived in the garden for a very long time. Little Tortoise, Simon Snail, Henry Hedgehog and Freddy Frog like to listen to his stories of days gone by.

MATERIALS FOR FREDDY FROG

- Double knitting yarn: 50 g light green and small amounts in white and black for features
- Pair of 3¼ mm (old size 10) knitting needles *or size to obtain correct tension*
- Good quality washable stuffing

FREDDY FROG

SIZE Freddy Frog measures approx 15.5 cm (6 in) in height, when worked in recommended tension

TENSION 27 sts and 38 rows to 10 cm (4 in) measured over st st and worked on 3¼ mm needles
Check your tension before beginning and change needle size if necessary.

BODY AND HEAD
With light green, cast on 25 sts.
1st row (RS) K into front and back of each st. (50 sts)
Starting with a P row, work 23 rows in st st, so ending with a P row.
NECK SHAPING
Next row (RS) (K2tog) 25 times. (25 sts)
P one row.
Next row K into front and back of each st. (50 sts)
P one row.
Next row *K1, K into front and back of next st, rep from * to end. (75 sts)
Starting with a P row, work 13 rows more in st st, so ending with a P row.
HEAD SHAPING
Next row (RS) *K1, K2tog, rep from * to end. (50 sts)
Starting with a P row, work 5 rows in st st, so ending with a P row.
Next row (RS) K25, turn leaving rem 25 sts unworked.
Next row P25.
Rep last 2 rows once more.
Next row (RS) (K2tog) 12 times, K1, turn.
Next row P13.
Next row (K2tog) 6 times, K1, turn.
Next row P7.

Break off yarn leaving a long loose end.

Using a blunt-ended needle, thread loose end through 7 sts just worked, pull yarn to gather tightly, then fasten off.

With RS facing, rejoin yarn to rem sts on needle and starting with a K row, work 4 rows in st st, so ending with a P row.

Next row (RS) (K2tog) 12 times, K1. (13 sts)

Next row P to end.

Next row (K2tog) 6 times, K1, turn. (7 sts)

Next row P to end.

Break off yarn leaving a long loose end and fasten off as for first side of head.

ARMS (make 2)

With light green, cast on 8 sts.

Starting with a K row, work 10 rows in st st, so ending with a P row.

**Next row (RS) K2tog, K4, K2tog. (6 sts)

P one row.

Next row K into front and back of first st, K4, K into front and back of last st. (8 sts)**

Starting with a P row, work 5 rows in st st, so ending with a P row.

Next row (RS) K1, (yfwd, K2tog) 3 times, K1. (8 sts)

Starting with a P row, work 5 rows in st st, so ending with a P row.

Rep from ** to ** once.

Starting with a K row, work 10 rows in st st. Cast off.

FEET (make 2)

With light green, cast on 12 sts.

Starting with a K row, work 10 rows in st st, so ending with a P row.

Next row (RS) K1, (yfwd, K2tog) 5 times, K1. (12 sts)

Starting with a P row, work 10 rows in st st. Cast off.

EYES (make 2)

With white, cast on 20 sts.

K one row.

P one row.

Next row (K2tog) 10 times. (10 sts)

Break off yarn leaving a long loose end.

Using a blunt-ended needle, thread loose end through all 10 sts on needle, pull yarn to gather tightly, then fasten off.

FINISHING

Body and head Leaving lower edge of body open, join centre back (row ends) of body and head up to where head divides in two, then join each top of head seam. Turn right side out.

Stuff body and head firmly. Oversew cast-on edge every alternate st, pull yarn to gather tightly and fasten off.

To shape neck wrap a length of light green yarn twice round the neck between the dec and inc rows. Pull yarn tightly to gather neck, knot at centre back neck and sew ends into neck.

To shape top of head begin at centre back and work running st round head along dec row. Pull ends to gather tightly, knot and sew ends of yarn into head.

Arms Fold arms in half along holes with wrong sides together.

Leaving cast-off and cast-on edge open, join side seams (row ends) and gather wrists through both layers with a running st. Stuff arms to wrist.

Oversew cast-on and cast-off edges tog, keeping seams at sides. Sew one arm to each side of body.

Feet Fold feet in half along holes with wrong sides tog. Join side seams (row ends) and oversew cast-on and cast-off edges tog, keeping seams at sides. Do not stuff. Sew feet to bottom of body with uneven edge facing forward.

Eyes Join row ends of eyes. Sew eyes to head so that they are touching at centre front and so that centres of eyes are lined up with dec row.

Embroidery Using black yarn, embroider pupils (see page 10).

Still using black, work two short vertical straight sts for nose and work mouth in back-stitch (as shown in the photograph).

Below: Freddy Frog and Simon Snail

MATERIALS FOR SIMON SNAIL

- Double knitting yarn: 40 g pink for body, 25 g grey for shell, 25 g light blue for hat
- Small amounts of double knitting yarn in bright yellow for hair, red for features, black for eyes and light yellow, red, mid-blue and green for flowers and leaves
- Pair of 3¼ mm (old size 10) knitting needles *or size to obtain correct tension*
- Good quality washable stuffing
- Red pencil for cheeks

SIMON SNAIL

SIZE Simon Snail measures approx 18 cm (7 in) in length, when worked in recommended tension

TENSION As for Freddy Frog

BODY AND HEAD

With pink, cast on 8 sts.

1st row (RS) K into front and back of each st. (16 sts)

2nd row P into front and back of each st. (32 sts)

Starting with a K row, work 46 rows in st st, so ending with a P row.

NECK SHAPING

Next row (RS) *K1, K into front and back of next st, rep from * to end. (48 sts)

Starting with a P row, work 20 rows in st st, so ending with a K row.

Next row (WS) (P2tog) 24 times. (24 sts)

Next row (K2tog) 12 times. (12 sts)

Break off yarn leaving a long loose end.

Using a blunt-ended needle, thread loose end through all 12 sts on needle, pull yarn to gather tightly, then fasten off.

SHELL

The shell is made in 3 separate pieces.

FIRST PIECE

With grey, cast on 15 sts.

**1st row (RS) K into front and back of each st. (30 sts)

Starting with a P row, work 15 rows in st st, so ending with a P row.

Next row (RS) (K2tog) 15 times. (15 sts)

Break off yarn leaving a long loose end.

Using a blunt-ended needle, thread loose end through all 15 sts on needle, pull yarn to gather tightly, then fasten off.**

SECOND PIECE

With grey, cast on 20 sts.

***1st row (RS) K into front and back of each st. (40 sts)

Starting with a P row, work 20 rows in st st, so ending with a K row.

Next row (WS) (P2tog) 20 times. (20 sts)

Break off yarn leaving a long loose end and fasten off as for first piece.***

THIRD PIECE

With grey, cast on 25 sts.

1st row (RS) K into front and back of each st. (50 sts)

Starting with a P row, work 25 rows in st st, so ending with a P row.

Next row (RS) (K2tog) 25 times. (25 sts)

Break off yarn leaving a long loose end and fasten off as for first piece.

HAT

The hat is made in 2 separate pieces.

FIRST PIECE

With light blue, cast on 15 sts.

Work as for first piece of shell from ** to **.

SECOND PIECE

With light blue, cast on 20 sts.

Work as for second piece of shell from *** to ***.

FLOWERS (make 3)

With red, cast on 10 sts.

1st row (RS) (K2tog) 5 times. (5 sts)

Break off yarn leaving a long loose end.

Using a blunt-ended needle, thread loose end through all 5 sts on needle, pull yarn to gather tightly, then fasten off.

Make 2 more flowers in the same way, but work one in mid-blue and one in light yellow.

LEAVES (make 3)

With green, cast on 3 sts.

K one row.

P one row.

Cast off.

FINISHING

Body and head Join centre back seam (row ends) of body and head, leaving opening at cast-on end large enough to stuff. Turn right side out.

Stuff body and head firmly. Complete centre back seam and oversew cast-on edge every alternate st, pull yarn to gather tightly and fasten off.

To shape neck wrap a length of pink yarn twice round the neck between the dec and inc rows. Pull yarn tightly to gather neck, knot at centre back neck and sew ends into neck.

Shell Join row ends of first shell piece, leaving cast-on edge open. Turn right side out.

Stuff first shell piece firmly. Oversew cast-on edge every alternate st, pull yarn to gather tightly and fasten off. Finish second and third shell pieces in same way. Then sew shell pieces tog, placing one on top of the other with the largest at the bottom and the smallest at the top.

Sew completed shell to back of body just below neckline and over centre back seam. Pull head back towards shell and secure to middle piece of shell with a few stitches.

Hat Finish hat pieces as for shell pieces, but do not stuff larger piece and stuff smaller piece only lightly. Sew stuffed piece to centre of unstuffed piece to form a brim on hat.

Using bright yellow, sew flowers to hat, stitching through centre to form centres on flowers. Sew on leaves close to flowers.

Hair Loop bright yellow yarn 20 times round four fingers and tie tog at centre. Sew loops of yarn to head, spreading loops out in a circle to cover entire head. Then sew hat to head with flowers at front.

Embroidery Using a single 'ply' of red yarn and working in backstitch, work a semi-circle for the mouth.

Using a single 'ply' of red yarn, work a short horizontal straight st and work twice over same st for nose.

Using black yarn, embroider eyes (see page 10) and colour cheeks with red pencil.

MATERIALS FOR BIG TORTOISE

- Double knitting yarn: 25 g in light yellow for body, 25 g pink for head, feet and tail
- Small amounts of double knitting yarn in bright yellow for hair, black for eyes and red for mouth and nose
- Pair of 3¼ mm (old size 10) knitting needles *or size to obtain correct tension*
- Good quality washable stuffing
- Red pencil for cheeks

MATERIALS FOR LITTLE TORTOISE

- Double knitting yarn: small amounts in yellow for body, pink for head and feet, and red and black for features
- Pair of 3¼ mm (old size 10) knitting needles *or size to obtain correct tension*
- Good quality washable stuffing
- Red pencil for cheeks

TORTOISES

SIZE Big Tortoise measures approx 15 cm (6 in) in length (including tail), when worked in recommended tension. Little Tortoise measures approx 7.5 cm (3 in) in length, when worked in recommended tension

TENSION As for Freddy Frog

BIG TORTOISE

BODY

With light yellow, cast on 30 sts.

1st row (RS) K into front and back of each st. (60 sts)

Starting with a P row, work 30 rows in st st, so ending with a K row.

Next row (WS) (P2tog) 30 times. (30 sts)

Next row (K2tog) 15 times. (15 sts)

Break off yarn leaving a long loose end.

Using a blunt-ended needle, thread loose end through all 15 sts on needle, pull yarn to gather tightly, then fasten off.

HEAD

With pink, cast on 15 sts.

1st row (RS) K into front and back of each st. (30 sts)

Starting with a P row, work 15 rows in st st, so ending with a P row.

Next row (RS) (K2tog) 15 times. (15 sts)

P one row.

Next row (K2tog) 7 times, K1. (8 sts)

Break off yarn leaving a long loose end and fasten off as for body.

FEET (make 4)

With pink, cast on 10 sts.

Starting with a K row, work 10 rows in st st, so ending with a P row.

Next row (RS) (K2tog) 5 times. (5 sts)

P one row.

Next row K into front and back of each st. (10 sts)

Starting with a P row, work 10 rows in st st, so ending with a K row.

Cast off purlwise.

TAIL

With pink, cast on 4 sts.

K one row.

P one row.

**Next row K into front and back of first st, K to last st, K into front and back of last st.

P one row.**

Rep from ** to ** 4 times more. (14 sts)

Cast off.

FINISHING

Body Join body seam (row ends), leaving bottom (cast-on) edge open. Turn right side out.

Stuff body lightly. Oversew cast-on edge every alternate st, pull yarn to gather tightly and fasten off.

Head Join head seam (row ends), leaving cast-on edge open. Turn right side out.

Stuff head firmly and oversew cast-on edge, keeping seam at centre. Sew head to side of body with seam at bottom.

Feet Fold one foot in half along row between inc and dec row, with right sides tog. Join side seam (row ends) on first side of foot and when fold is reached, secure yarn but do not break

Henry Hedgehog

Little Tortoise

Big Tortoise

off. Now work a running st along fold, pull yarn to gather slightly and secure yarn, then continue seam along other side of foot. Turn foot right side out.

Sew other feet tog in same way. Stuff each foot firmly and oversew cast-on and cast-off edges tog. Sew two feet to each side of body.

Tail Join tail seam (row ends), leaving cast-on edge open. Turn right side out, stuff firmly and oversew cast-on edge, keeping seam at centre. Sew tail to end of body with seam at bottom.

Hair Wrap bright yellow yarn about 23 times round a 5 cm (2 in) piece of card. Slip looped yarn carefully off card, keeping it folded in half and tie at centre with a separate length of bright yellow yarn. Sew tied section to centre of top of head and spread loops out in a circle. Trim ends to form an even circle.

Embroidery Using a single 'ply' of red yarn, work a semi-circle in backstitch for mouth.

Using a single 'ply' of red yarn, work a short horizontal straight st and work twice over same st for nose.

Using black yarn, embroider eyes (see page 10) and colour cheeks with red pencil.

LITTLE TORTOISE

BODY AND HEAD
With yellow, cast on 16 sts.
1st row (RS) K into front and back of each st. (32 sts)
Starting with a P row, work 15 rows in st st, so ending with a P row.

HENRY HEDGEHOG

SIZE Hedgehog measures approx 7.5 cm (3 in) in length, when worked in recommended tension

TENSION As for Freddy Frog

BODY AND HEAD
With dark brown, cast on 16 sts.
Inc row (RS) K into front and back of each st. (32 sts)
1st patt row (WS) P1, K1, rep from * to end.
2nd patt row K1, P1.
Rep last 2 rows 6 times more, then rep first patt row once more.

NECK SHAPING
Next row (RS) (K2tog) 16 times. (16 sts)
P one row.
Break off yellow and change to pink for head.
**Starting with a K row, work 10 rows in st st, so ending with a P row.
Next row (RS) (K2tog) 8 times. (8 sts)
Break off yarn leaving a long loose end.
Using a blunt-ended needle, thread loose end through all 8 sts on needle, pull yarn to gather tightly, then fasten off.**

FEET (make 4)
With pink, cast on 4 sts.
Starting with a K row, work 12 rows in st st.
Cast off.

FINISHING
Body and head Join seam (row ends) of body and head, leaving bottom (cast-on) edge open. Turn right side out.

Stuff body and head firmly. Oversew cast-on edge every alternate st, pull yarn to gather tightly and fasten off.

To shape neck wrap a length of yellow yarn once round neck at last yellow row. Pull yarn tightly to gather neck, knot at seam and sew ends into neck.

Feet Fold feet in half between the sixth and seventh rows with wrong sides tog. Join side seams (row ends) and oversew cast-on and cast-off edges tog. Do not stuff.

Sew two feet to each side of body.

Embroidery Work mouth, nose and eyes as for Big Tortoise. Colour cheeks with red pencil.

NECK SHAPING
Next row (RS) (K2tog) 16 times. (16 sts)
P one row.
Break off dark brown and change to light brown for head.
Complete as for Little Tortoise as given above from ** to **.

FEET (make 4)
Work as for Little Tortoise, but use light brown instead of pink.

FINISHING
Finish as for Little Tortoise, but work all features in black and do not shape neck.

MATERIALS FOR HENRY HEDGEHOG
- Double knitting yarn: small amounts in dark brown for body, light brown for head and feet, black for features
- Pair of 3¼ mm (old size 10) knitting needles *or size to obtain correct tension*
- Good quality washable stuffing
- Red pencil for cheeks

FAIRY TALES AND NURSERY Rhymes

LITTLE RED RIDING HOOD

★ ★

Granny had been feeling poorly so Little Red Riding Hood set off to visit her with a basket of goodies. A big bad Wolf was lying in wait.

MATERIALS FOR RED RIDING HOOD

- Double knitting yarn: 50 g pink for arms, legs and head, 50 g light blue for body and smock, 25 g black for shoes, 25 g mid-blue for smock, 50 g red for cape, 25 g light brown for hair and basket
- Small amounts of double knitting yarn in white for socks and random-dyed yarn for basket cover
- Pair of 3¼ mm (old size 10) knitting needles *or size to obtain correct tension*
- Good quality washable stuffing
- Red pencil for cheeks

RED RIDING HOOD

SIZE Red Riding Hood measures approx 25.5 cm (10 in) in height, when worked in recommended tension

TENSION 27 sts and 38 rows to 10 cm (4 in) measured over st st and worked on 3¼ mm needles
Check your tension before beginning and change needle size if necessary.

DOLL

TO MAKE
Work body and head, arms and legs as for Goldilocks (see pages 94-96), but use light blue for white on body.

FINISHING
Finish and stuff body and head, legs and arms as for Goldilocks, but using a length of light blue yarn to shape neck.
Do not sew arms to body until smock has been completed.
Hair Loosely wrap light brown yarn about 40 times round a 20 cm (8 in) piece of card. Slip looped yarn carefully off card, keeping it folded in half. Wrap a separate length of light brown yarn round the centre of the looped yarn, so that each group of looped ends measures 10 cm (4 in), pull tightly and knot.
Sew the tied section to the centre of back of head and evenly spread out the loops to cover the head. Sew the hair in place by working backstitch 3 cm (1 in) from the looped ends all round the head, forming a fringe of loops around the face and back of head at neck.

Embroidery Using a single 'ply' of red yarn and working in backstitch, work a semi-circle for the mouth.

Using a single 'ply' of red yarn, work a short horizontal straight st and work twice over same st for nose.

Using black yarn, embroider the eyes (see the instructions on page 10).

Colour cheeks with red pencil.

SMOCK

SKIRT
Work as for Goldilocks, but use light blue for white, and mid-blue for dark blue.

SLEEVES (make 2)
With mid-blue, cast on 21 sts.
K 2 rows (garter st).
Starting with a P row, work 25 rows in st st, so ending with a P row.
Next row (RS) (K2tog) 10 times, K1. (11 sts)
Break off yarn leaving a long loose end.
Using a blunt-ended needle, thread loose end through all 11 sts on needle, pull yarn to gather tightly, then fasten off.

FINISHING
Sleeves and arms Finish sleeves, insert arms and join to body as for Goldilocks.
Skirt Join centre back seam (row ends) of skirt and turn right side out.

Using light blue yarn, work a line of running st along waist of skirt one row from cast-on edge leaving long loose ends. Slip skirt onto doll, positioning waistline 2 cm (¾ in) below neck, pull yarn to gather skirt and sew skirt in place.

Right: Detail of Little Red Riding Hood's head and shoulders

CAPE

TO MAKE
With red, cast on 70 sts.
K 4 rows (garter st).
Next row (WS) K2, P66, K2.
****K one row.
Next row K2, P66, K2.**
Rep from ** to ** 13 times more.
NECK SHAPING
Next row (RS) K2, (K2tog) 33 times, K2. (37 sts)
*****Next row** K2, P33, K2.
K one row.***
Rep from *** to *** 12 times more.
Next row (WS) K2, P10, (P2tog) 3 times, P1, (P2tog) 3 times, P10, K2.
Cast off rem 31 sts.

FINISHING
Fold cast-off edge of hood in half with wrong sides tog and join top of hood seam. Turn right side out.

Using red yarn, work a running st along dec row of cape, leaving a long loose end at each end of row for ties. Put hood on doll's head and tie a bow at front neck with loose ends.

BASKET

TO MAKE
With light brown, cast on 15 sts.
1st row (RS) K into front and back of each st. (30 sts)
Starting with a P row, work 9 rows in st st.
Cast off.

HANDLE
With light brown, cast on 25 sts.
K one row. Cast off.

BASKET COVER
With random-dyed yarn, cast on 10 sts.
Starting with a K row, work 10 rows in st st.
Cast off.

FINISHING
Oversew cast-on edge of basket on every alternate st, pull yarn to gather tightly, then join seam (row ends) and turn right side out.

Sew ends of handle to top edge of basket. Stuff basket and sew basket cover firmly in place over stuffing. Sew handle to doll's hand.

MATERIALS FOR GRANNY

- Double knitting yarn: 50 g pink for arms, legs and head, 75 g dark pink for body and dress, 25 g white for apron, 25 g black for shoes, 25 g light brown for hair
- Small amounts of double knitting yarn in red for features and mid-blue for trim
- Pair of 3¼ mm (old size 10) knitting needles *or size to obtain correct tension*
- Good quality washable stuffing
- Red pencil for cheeks

GRANNY

SIZE As for Red Riding Hood

TENSION As for Red Riding Hood

DOLL

BODY AND HEAD

Work as for Goldilocks (see page 94), but use dark pink for white.

ARMS

Work as for Goldilocks.

LEGS (make 2)

With pink, cast on 20 sts.
Starting with a K row, work 24 rows in st st, so ending with a P row.
Break off pink yarn and change to black to make shoes.
Complete shoes as for Goldilocks from ** to **.

FINISHING

Finish and stuff body and head, legs and arms as for Goldilocks, but using a length of dark pink yarn to shape neck.

Do not sew arms to body until dress has been completed.

Hair Loosely wrap light brown yarn about 40 times round a 10 cm (4 in) piece of card. Slip looped yarn carefully off card, keeping it folded in half. Wrap a separate length of light brown yarn round the centre of the looped yarn, so that each group of looped ends measures 5 cm (2 in), pull tightly and knot.

Sew the tied section to the centre of the back of the head and evenly spread out the loops to cover the head. Sew the hair in place by working backstitch along the looped ends all round the head (these ends will be covered by bunched curls).

For bunched curls, loosely wrap light brown yarn about 26 times round a 3 cm (1¼ in) piece of card. Slip off card and tie at centre as for main hair. Make eleven more bunches in the same way. Sew curls all round head covering loop ends already stitched in place.

Embroidery Work mouth, nose, eyes, and cheeks as for Red Riding Hood.

Then using a single 'ply' of black yarn, work spectacles in backstitch.

DRESS

SKIRT

With dark pink, cast on 60 sts.
K one row.
P one row.
Next row (RS) *K1, K into front and back of next st, rep from * to end. (90 sts)
Starting with a P row, work 34 rows in st st, so ending with a K row.
K 3 rows (garter st).
Cast off.

SLEEVES

Work as for Red Riding Hood, but use dark pink instead of mid-blue.

FINISHING

Sleeves and arms Finish sleeves, insert arms and join to body as for Goldilocks.
Skirt Join centre back seam (row ends) of skirt and turn right side out.

Using mid-blue yarn, work a line of running st along bottom of skirt one row above garter st edge. Then using dark pink yarn, work a line of running st along waist of skirt one row from cast-on edge leaving long loose ends. Slip skirt onto doll positioning waistline 5 cm (2 in) below neck, pull yarn to gather top of skirt, tie ends and sew skirt in place.

Using mid-blue yarn, make a small bow and sew to centre front neck.

Using mid-blue yarn, embroider three short (doubled) horizontal sts below bow down bodice for 'buttons'.

APRON

TO MAKE

With white, cast on 30 sts.
K 4 rows (garter st).
Next row (WS) K2, P26, K2.
**K one row.
Next row K2, P26, K2.**
Rep from ** to ** 7 times more.
Cast on 20 sts at end of last row. (50 sts)
Next row (RS) K20, (K1, K2tog) 10 times. (40 sts)
Cast on 20 sts at end of last row. (60 sts)
K 2 rows (garter st).
Cast off.
Tie apron in place on doll.

MATERIALS FOR WOLF

- Double knitting yarn: 75 g in light brown and small amount in black for features
- Pair of 3¼ mm (old size 10) knitting needles *or size to obtain correct tension*
- Good quality washable stuffing

Right: To make a knotted eye, wind one end of yarn round the other several times, then pull both ends to form an oval shape

WOLF

SIZE The Wolf measures approx 21.5 cm (8½ in) in height (including ears), when worked in recommended tension

TENSION As for Red Riding Hood

BODY AND HEAD
With light brown, cast on 33 sts.
1st row (RS) K into front and back of each st. (66 sts)
Starting with a P row, work 35 rows in st st, so ending with a P row.
NECK SHAPING
Next row (RS) (K2tog) 33 times. (33 sts)
P one row.
Next row K into front and back of each st. (66 sts)
HEAD SHAPING
Next row P32, (P into front and back of next st) twice, P32. (68 sts)
Next row K33, (K into front and back of next st) twice, K33. (70 sts)
**Next row P to 2 centre sts, P into front and back of each of 2 centre sts, P to end.
Next row K to 2 centre sts, K into front and back of each of 2 centre sts, K to end.**
Rep from ** to ** twice more. (82 sts)
Starting with a P row, work 2 rows in st st, so ending with a K row.
Next row P39, (P2tog) twice, P39. (80 sts)
Next row K38, (K2tog) twice, K38. (78 sts)
***Next row P to 4 centre sts, (P2tog) twice, P to end.
Next row K to 4 centre sts, (K2tog) twice, K to end.***
Rep from *** to *** twice more. (66 sts)
Starting with a P row, work 7 rows in st st, so ending with a P row.

Next row (RS) (K2tog) 33 times. (33 sts)
Next row P1, (P2tog) 16 times. (17 sts)
Next row K1, (K2tog) 8 times. (9 sts)
Break off yarn leaving a long loose end.
Using a blunt-ended needle, thread loose end through all 9 sts on needle, pull yarn to gather tightly, then fasten off.

ARMS (make 2)
With light brown, cast on 12 sts.
Starting with a K row, work 18 rows in st st, so ending with a P row.
Next row (RS) (K2tog) 6 times. (6 sts)
P one row.
Next row K into front and back of each st. (12 sts)
Starting with a P row, work 18 rows in st st, so ending with a K row.
Cast off purlwise.

FEET (make 2)
With light brown, cast on 12 sts.
Starting with a K row, work 12 rows in st st, so ending with a P row.
Next row (RS) (K2tog) 6 times. (6 sts)
P one row.
Next row K into front and back of each st. (12 sts)
Starting with a P row, work 12 rows in st st, so ending with a K row.
Cast off purlwise.

EARS (make 2)
With light brown, cast on 16 sts.
Starting with a K row, work 16 rows in st st.
Cast off.

TAIL
With light brown, cast on 10 sts.
K one row.
**Next row (WS) *Insert right-hand needle knitwise in next st, wind yarn clockwise round point of needle, first finger of left hand and over point of needle again, draw the 2 loops on needle through, rep from * to end.
Next row K to end, treating each double loop as a single st and pulling loops down firmly. (10 sts)**
Rep from ** to ** 16 times more.
Break off yarn leaving a long loose end.
Using a blunt-ended needle, thread loose end through all 10 sts on needle, pull yarn to gather tightly, then fasten off.

FINISHING

Body and head Finish and stuff body and head as for Bears (see page 98).

Feet and arms Finish, stuff and sew onto body as for legs and arms of Bears.

Ears Fold Wolf's ears in half diagonally with wrong sides tog to form triangles. Oversew both sides tog.

Sew the ears to the top of the head, with the folded edge facing outwards.

Tail Fold tail in half lengthways with wrong sides tog and oversew all three sides tog. Sew tail to bottom centre back of wolf.

Embroidery Using one strand of black yarn and working in satin st, work a round nose at end of point on head. Still using black, work a V-shaped mouth.

Using black yarn, embroider eyes. Mark eye positions with a pin and cut a strand of black yarn. Make a loose knot and wind yarn around several times (see Fig. a on opposite page). Pull ends to tighten knot (see Fig. b).

Using a blunt-ended needle, pass yarn ends through eye position, exiting at arm position. Pull ends so knot touches face, fasten and trim. Repeat for second eye.

Above: *Wolf, Granny and Little Red Riding Hood*

SNOW WHITE AND THE SEVEN DWARFS

♥ ♥

'Mirror, Mirror on the wall, who is the fairest of them all?' 'Snow White, of course!' the Seven Dwarfs clamour in unison.

MATERIALS FOR SNOW WHITE

- Double knitting yarn: 50 g pink for arms, legs and head, 25 g dark blue for body, 25 g mid-blue for sleeves, 25 g yellow for skirt, 50 g black for hair and shoes
- Small amount of double knitting yarn in red for features, hair bow and sleeve trim
- Pair of 3¼ mm (old size 10) knitting needles *or size to obtain correct tension*
- Good quality washable stuffing
- Red pencil for cheeks

SNOW WHITE

SIZE Snow White measures approx 25.5 cm (10 in) in height, when worked in recommended tension

TENSION 27 sts and 38 rows to 10 cm (4 in) measured over st st and worked on 3¼ mm needles
Check your tension before beginning and change needle size if necessary.

DOLL

TO MAKE
Work body and head, and arms as for Goldilocks (see pages 94-96), but use dark blue for white on body. Work legs as for Granny (see page 87).

FINISHING
Body and head Finish and stuff body and head, legs and arms as for Goldilocks, but using a length of dark blue yarn to shape neck. (Do not sew arms to body until dress is completed.)
Hair Cut fifty 23 cm (9 in) lengths and sixty-five 33 cm (13 in) lengths of black yarn. Holding shorter lengths tog, wrap a separate length of black yarn round centre and tie. Sew the tied section to the top of the head so that the cut ends hang down over sides of head. Then holding longer lengths tog, fold in half and tie 4 cm (1½ in) from folded end. Sew to top of head so that folded end forms fringe and cut ends hang down over back of head. Make a red twisted cord and tie round head into a bow.
Embroidery Using a single 'ply' of red yarn, work a V-shaped mouth.

Using a single 'ply' of red yarn, work an upside down smaller V for nose.

Using black yarn, embroider eyes (see instructions given on page 10).

Colour cheeks with red pencil.

DRESS

TO MAKE

With yellow, work skirt as for Granny (see page 87) and with mid-blue, work sleeves as for Goldilocks (see page 97).

MATERIALS FOR DWARFS

- Double knitting yarn: 100 g pink for heads and arms, 40 g each dark green, mid-blue, light blue, maroon, red, dark blue and sea green for bodies and hats, 25 g light brown for belts, 50 g black for feet
- Small amounts of double knitting yarn in brown for hair, in yellow for buckles and hair, and in white for beards
- Pair of 3¼ mm (old size 10) knitting needles *or size to obtain correct tension*
- 3 mm crochet hook for beards
- Good quality washable stuffing
- Red pencil for cheeks

SEVEN DWARFS

SIZE Each Dwarf measures approx 14 cm (5½ in) in height, when worked in recommended tension

TENSION As for Snow White

DWARFS

BODY AND HEAD

The dwarfs are all made in the same way, but each dwarf is worked with a different body colour. Use sea green for No. 1, dark blue for No. 2, light blue for No. 3, red for No. 4, mid-blue for No. 5, maroon for No. 6 and dark green for No. 7.

With body colour, cast on 25 sts.

1st row (RS) K into front and back of each st. (50 sts)

Starting with a P row, work 12 rows in st st, so ending with a K row.

Break off body colour and change to light brown for belt.

P 2 rows.

K one row (WS).

Break off light brown and change back to body colour.

Complete as for Roley Poley Kids (see pages 36-38) from ** to **.

ARMS AND FEET

Work as for Roley Poley Kids.

SLEEVES

With same colour as body colour, work as for long sleeves for Roley Poley Kids.

FINISHING

Sleeves and arms Finish sleeves, insert arms and join to body as for Goldilocks.

Then using red yarn, work 1 cm (¼ in) long vertical straight sts (2 knit sts apart) all round sleeve 1 cm (¼ in) from cast-on edge.

Skirt Join centre back seam (row ends) of skirt. Turn right side out and using yellow yarn, work a line of running st along waist of skirt one row from cast-on edge leaving long loose ends.

Slip skirt onto doll positioning waistline 5 cm (2 in) below neck, pull yarn to gather top of skirt, tie ends and sew skirt in place.

HAT (make 2 pieces)
With same colour as body colour, cast on 26 sts.
K 4 rows (garter st).
P one row.
***Next row** (RS) K2tog, K to last 2 sts, K2tog.
P one row.***
Rep from *** to *** 10 times more. (4 sts rem)
Next row (K2tog) twice. (2 sts)
Next row P2tog.
Fasten off.

FINISHING

Finish and stuff body and head, and finish feet and attach as for Roley Poley Kids. Finish arms and sleeves, and sew to body as for The Roley Poley Kids.

Note: Add a little extra stuffing to body and head of No. 2.

Hats Join two pieces of hats (row ends) tog.
Hair For No. 7 work a few loops of white yarn to stick out from under hat at centre of forehead. Work hair for No. 2 and No. 6 in the same way but with yellow yarn.

For No. 3 work hair as for No. 7 but with brown and then work a few loops in the same way to stick out from under hat at each side of the head.

For No. 4 work loops of yellow yarn to stick out from under hat all along forehead.

Omit hair on No. 1 and No. 5. Sew hats to matching bodies, with seams at sides of head.
Beards Work beards for No. 1, No. 5 and No. 7. Cut about forty 10 cm (4 in) lengths of white yarn for each beard. Fold one length in half over end of crochet hook and 'tie' folded length onto a separate piece of white yarn 30 cm (12 in)

Above: *The Seven Dwarfs*

1   2   3   4

5   6   7

long by drawing cut ends through loop on hook and around longer piece and pulling tightly (see diagram). Work fringe onto 30 cm (12 in) length of yarn in this way until fringe is long enough to fit from 'ear' to 'ear' of dwarf. Sew fringe firmly to dwarf and trim beard to 2 cm (¾ in).

Embroidery Using black yarn, embroider eyes (see instructions for knotted eyes on page 10) in the same way for all the dwarfs except No. 3. For No. 3 work V-shaped eyes with a single 'ply' of black yarn. Also using a single 'ply' of black, work slanting eyebrows for No. 5 to create a frown, and work backstitch spectacles on No. 7.

Use a single 'ply' of red yarn for all mouths and noses. For No.1, No. 2 and No. 7 work a V-shaped mouth. For No. 5's mouth work an upside down V. For No. 6 work a larger semi-circular mouth using backstitch. For No. 3 work only a short straight horizontal stitch for mouth. For No. 4 work a V-shaped mouth with a tiny straight stitch perpendicular added to each end of the V.

For all noses (except for No. 6) work a doubled straight horizontal st, using a single 'ply' of red yarn. Work nose for No. 6 as for eyes, but with red and worked horizontally.

With yellow yarn, work a buttonhole stitch to form the buckle on each belt (see the diagram on page 40).

Colour the cheeks of all Seven Dwarfs with red pencil (see instructions on page 11).

Below: *'Tie' folded pieces of yarn onto a separate length of yarn to form a beard*

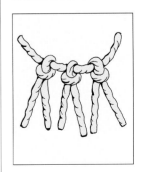

GOLDILOCKS AND THE THREE BEARS

The Three Bears were extremely fond of their porridge, so when Goldilocks helped herself to their breakfast they were none too pleased.

MATERIALS FOR GOLDILOCKS

- Double knitting yarn:
  50 g pink for arms,
  legs and head, 50 g
  white for body, smock
  and socks,
  25 g black for shoes,
  25 g dark blue for
  smock, 25 g yellow
  for hair
- Small amounts of
  double knitting yarn in
  red for mouth, green
  for hair bows, and
  mid-blue for trim
- Pair of 3¼ mm (old
  size 10) knitting
  needles *or size to
  obtain correct tension*
- Good quality washable
  stuffing
- Red pencil for cheeks

GOLDILOCKS

SIZE Goldilocks measures approx 25.5 cm (10 in) in height, when worked in recommended tension

TENSION 27 sts and 38 rows to 10 cm (4 in) measured over st st and worked on 3¼ mm needles
Check your tension before beginning and change needle size if necessary.

DOLL

BODY AND HEAD
With white, cast on 40 sts.
Starting with a K row, work 26 rows in st st, so ending with a P row.
NECK SHAPING
Next row (RS) (K2tog) 20 times. (20 sts)
P one row.
Break off white and change to pink for head.
Next row (RS) K into front and back of each st. (40 sts)
Starting with a P row, work 19 rows more in st st, so ending with a P row.
Next row (RS) (K2tog) 20 times. (20 sts)
P one row.
Next row (K2tog) 10 times. (10 sts)
Break off yarn leaving a long loose end.
Using a blunt-ended needle, thread loose end through all 10 sts on needle, pull yarn to gather tightly, then fasten off.

ARMS (make 2)
With pink, cast on 14 sts.
Starting with a K row, work 34 rows in st st, so ending with a P row.

Next row (RS) (K2tog) 7 times. (7 sts)
Break off yarn leaving a long loose end and
fasten off as for body and head.

LEGS (make 2)
With pink, cast on 20 sts.
Starting with a K row, work 18 rows in st st,
so ending with a P row.
Break off pink and change to white for socks.
K 3 rows (garter st).
Starting with a P row, work 3 rows in st st,
so ending with a P row.
Break off white and change to black for shoes.
**K 2 rows (garter st).
Next row (RS) K7, *(K1, P1 and K1) all into next
st to make 2 extra sts*, rep from * to * 5 times
more, K7. (32 sts)
Starting with a P row, work 7 rows in st st,
so ending with a P row.
Next row (RS) (K2tog) 16 times. (16 sts)
P one row.
Next row (K2tog) 8 times. (8 sts)
Break off yarn leaving a long loose end.
Using a blunt-ended needle, thread loose end
through all 8 sts on needle, pull yarn to gather
tightly, then fasten off.††

FINISHING
Body and head Join centre back seam (row
ends) of body and head, using matching yarn
for each section and leaving cast-on edge of
body open. Turn right side out.
Stuff body and head firmly. Oversew cast-on
edge of body tog keeping seam at centre back.
To shape neck wrap a length of white yarn
twice round the neck between the dec and inc
rows. Pull yarn tightly to gather neck, knot at
centre back neck and sew ends into neck.
Legs Join centre back (row ends) of each leg,
using matching yarn for each section and
leaving top edge of each leg open. Turn legs
right side out.
Stuff each leg firmly and oversew top edge
tog, keeping seam at centre back. Sew legs to
lower edge of body.
Arms Join arm seams (row ends), leaving top
of each arm open. Turn arms right side out.
Stuff each arm firmly and oversew top edge
tog, keeping seam at centre.
To shape wrist wrap a length of pink yarn
once round arm about 10 rows from gathered
end. Pull yarn tightly to gather wrist, knot at
seam and sew ends into seam.

Goldilocks

Do not sew arms to body until smock has been completed.

Hair Loosely wrap yellow yarn about 30 times round a 25 cm (10 in) piece of card. Slip looped yarn carefully off card, keeping it folded in half. Wrap a separate length of yellow yarn round strands 3 cm (1¼ in) from one folded end, pull tightly and knot (see Fig. a). Cut strands along the fold at the other end and part in two so that the cut ends hang down either side of the face. Sew tied section to top of head so that folded loops fall over forehead to form fringe and sew in place (see Fig. b).

Wrap yellow yarn about 50 times round a 25 cm (10 in) piece of card. Slip looped yarn off the card and cut along fold at one end. Lay strands over back of head so that they cover head from tied section of fringe to back of neck and so that the centre of the strands lie along a centre parting. To secure in place work backstitch from tied section of fringe to centre back neck, forming a hair parting (see Fig. c).

Plait hair each side, trim and tie with green yarn bows. Secure the plaits to both sides of the head with a few stitches (Fig. d).

Embroidery Using a single 'ply' of red yarn, work a V-shaped mouth.

Using black yarn make eyes (see page 10).

Using pink yarn, embroider nose as for eyes but work horizontally.

Colour cheeks with red pencil.

SMOCK

SKIRT

With white, cast on 60 sts.

K one row.

P one row.

Next row (RS) *K1, K into front and back of next st, rep from * to end. (90 sts)

Starting with a P row, work 22 rows in st st, so ending with a K (RS) row.

K one row.

Break off white and change to dark blue.

K one row.

P one row.

Next row (RS) *K5, K into front and back of next st, rep from * to end. (105 sts)

Starting with a P row, work 4 rows in st st, so ending with a K row.

K one row.

Cast off.

SLEEVES (make 2)

With dark blue, cast on 20 sts.

1st row (RS) K into front and back of each st. (40 sts)

Starting with a P row, work 9 rows in st st, so ending with a P row.

Next row (RS) (K2tog) 20 times. (20 sts)

P one row.

Next row (RS) (K2tog) 10 times. (10 sts)

Break off yarn leaving a long loose end.

Using a blunt-ended needle, thread loose end through all 10 sts on needle, pull yarn to gather tightly, then fasten off.

FINISHING

Sleeves and arms Join sleeve seams (row ends). Turn right side out.

Insert arms into sleeves with seams lined up, then sew ends of arms to sleeves. With sleeve seams facing body, sew one sleeve to each side of body just below neck.

Skirt Using a single 'ply' of mid-blue yarn, work a line of running st along waist of skirt one row from cast-on edge and another line at bottom of skirt along third to last row of white.

Join centre back seam (row ends) of skirt. Turn right side out. Put skirt on doll and sew in place just below sleeves and about 3 cm (1¼ in) below neck. Using a single 'ply' of mid-blue yarn, make a little bow and sew to centre front of doll just below neck.

Below: *For long hair, tie bunched loops of yarn at one end and cut along fold at other end, then stitch to forehead to form a fringe; cover back of head with long strands of yarn and secure with backstitch along centre parting; attach plaits to side of face with a few stitches*

MATERIALS FOR THREE BEARS

- Double knitting yarn: 100 g light brown and 50 g brown for bears
- Small amounts of double knitting yarn in black for features, and in white, light blue and cream for bowls of porridge
- Pair of 3¼ mm (old size 10) knitting needles *or size to obtain correct tension*
- Good quality washable stuffing
- Red pencil for cheeks
- Tin foil for spoons

THE THREE BEARS

SIZE Daddy and Mummy Bear each measure approx 15 cm (6 in) in height and Baby Bear measures approx 10 cm (4 in) in height when worked in recommended tension

TENSION As for Goldilocks

BEARS

BODY AND HEAD

Figures outside brackets are for Baby Bear.
Make Daddy and Mummy Bear in the same way, following instructions in brackets [ ].
With light brown, cast on 16 [25] sts.
1st row (RS) K into front and back of each st. (32 [50] sts)
Starting with a P row, work 15 [23] rows in st st, so ending with a P row.
NECK SHAPING
Next row (RS) (K2tog) 16 [25] times. (16 [25] sts)
P one row.
Next row K into front and back of each st. (32 [50] sts)
Starting with a P row, work 13 [21] rows in st st, so ending with a P row.
Next row (RS) (K2tog) 16 [25] times. (16 [25] sts)
Next row (P2tog) 8 [12] times, P0 [1]. (8 [13] sts)
Break off yarn leaving a long loose end.
Using a blunt-ended needle, thread loose end through all 8 [13] sts on needle, pull yarn to gather tightly, then fasten off.

ARMS (make 2)

With brown, cast on 7 [10] sts.
Starting with a K row, work 10 [14] rows in st st, so ending with a P row.
Next row (RS) (K2tog) 3 [5] times, K1 [0]. (4 [5] sts)
P one row.
Next row (K into front and back of next st) 3 [5] times, K1 [0]. (7 [10] sts)
Starting with a P row, work 10 [14] rows in st st, so ending with a K row.
Cast off purlwise.

LEGS (make 2)

Make legs in same way as for arms.

EARS (make 2)

With light brown, cast on 10 [14] sts.
Starting with a K row, work 6 [10] rows in st st, so ending with a P row.
Next row (RS) (K2tog) twice, K2 [6], (K2tog) twice. (6 [10] sts)
P one row.
Break off light brown and change to brown.
Starting with a K row, work 4 [8] rows in st st.
Cast off.

FINISHING

Body and head Join centre back seam (row ends) of body and head, leaving lower edge of body open. Turn right side out.

Stuff body and head firmly. Oversew cast-on edge every alternate st, pull yarn to gather tightly and fasten off.

To shape neck wrap a length of light brown yarn twice round the neck between the dec and inc rows. Pull the yarn tightly to gather the neck, knot at centre back neck and sew ends into the neck.

Legs Fold one leg in half along row between increase and decrease rows, with right sides tog. Join side seam (row ends) on first side of leg and when fold is reached, secure yarn but do not break off. Now work a running st along fold, pull yarn to gather slightly and secure yarn, then continue seam down other side of leg. Turn leg right side out.

Sew other leg tog in same way. Stuff each leg firmly and oversew top edge tog, keeping seams at sides.

Sew one leg to each side of lower body.
Arms Finish as for legs and sew one arm to each side of upper body just below neck.
Ears Make up as for legs, but do not stuff. Sew ears to top of head, with dark brown sides facing front.
Embroidery Using a single 'ply' of black double knitting yarn and working in satin st, make a circle for nose.

Using a single 'ply' of black double knitting yarn, work a short vertical straight st from centre of nose to centre of mouth. Work a straight st from centre of mouth slanting slightly upwards to the right, then work the other half of the mouth to the left in the same way to complete the V-shaped mouth.

Using black yarn, embroider eyes (see instructions on page 10).

Colour cheeks with red pencil.

BOWLS OF PORRIDGE

BOWLS (make 3)

With white, cast on 18 sts.

1st row (RS) K into front and back of each st. (36 sts)

With white, P one row.

**With light blue, K one row, P one row.

With white, K one row, P one row.**

Rep from ** to ** once.

With light blue, K 2 rows (garter st).

Break off light blue and change to white only for remainder of bowl.

Next row (RS) *K4, K2tog, rep from * to end. (30 sts)

Starting with a P row, work 5 rows in st st, so ending with a P row.

Next row (RS) (K2tog) 15 times. (15 sts)

P one row.

Next row (RS) (K2tog) 7 times, K1. (8 sts)

P one row.

Break off yarn leaving a long loose end.

Using a blunt-ended needle, thread loose end through all 8 sts on needle, pull yarn to gather tightly, then fasten off.

Make two more bowls in the same way as the first bowl.

PORRIDGE (make 3)

With cream, cast on 11 sts.

1st row (RS) K1, (P1, K1) 5 times.

Rep last row 13 times more.

Cast off.

Make two more porridge pieces in the same way as the first.

FINISHING

Join bowl seam (row ends), leaving ends open and turn right side out.

Oversew cast-on edge every alternate stitch, pull yarn to gather tightly, then place cast-off edge on top of cast-on edge just gathered and stitch firmly in place. The white side of the bowl is the inside.

Using cream yarn, work a running stitch all round edge of porridge and pull slightly to gather into a flat circle.

Stuff porridge lightly and sew to inside (white side) of bowl.

Shape three spoons from tin foil and sew one to top of each porridge bowl.

Note: Do not make the tin foil porridge spoons for young children (under three years of age), as they could easily present a choking hazard if swallowed.

Above: *The Three Bears*

JACK AND JILL

'Jack and Jill went up the hill to fetch a pail of water, Jack fell down and broke his crown and Jill came tumbling after.' These favourite nursery rhyme characters evoke all the old-fashioned, rustic charm of days gone by.

MATERIALS FOR JILL

· Double knitting yarn: 50 g pink for arms, legs and head, 50 g lilac for body and smock, 25 g black for shoes, 50 g maroon for smock and hat, 20 g light brown for hair
· Small amounts of double knitting yarn in red for features and white for socks
· Pair of 3¼ mm (old size 10) knitting needles or size to obtain correct tension
· Good quality washable stuffing
· Red pencil for cheeks

JILL

SIZE Jill measures approx 30 cm (12 in) in height, when worked in recommended tension

TENSION 27 sts and 38 rows to 10 cm (4 in) measured over st st using 3¼ mm needles
  Check your tension before beginning and change needle size if necessary.

DOLL

BODY AND HEAD
With lilac, cast on 56 sts.
Starting with a K row, work 32 rows in st st.
NECK SHAPING
Next row (RS) (K2tog) 28 times. (28 sts)
Break off lilac and change to pink for head.
P one row.
Next row K into front and back of each st. (56 sts)
Starting with a P row, work 27 row in st st.
Next row (RS) (K2tog) 28 times. (28 sts)
Next row (P2tog) 14 times. (14 sts)
Break off yarn leaving a long loose end.
Using a blunt-ended needle, thread loose end through all 14 sts on needle, pull yarn to gather tightly, then fasten off.

ARMS (make 2)
With pink, cast on 11 sts.
1st row (RS) K into front and back of each st. (22 sts)
Starting with a P row, work 35 rows in st st.
Next row (RS) (K2tog) 11 times. (11 sts)
Break off yarn leaving a long loose end and fasten off as for head.

LEGS (make 2)
With black, cast on 24 sts.

1st row (RS) K into front and back of each st. (48 sts)
Starting with a P row, work 13 rows in st st.
Next row (RS) K6, (K2tog) twice, (K3tog) 9 times, (K2tog) twice, K7. (26 sts)
K 3 rows (garter st).
Break off black and change to white.
Starting with a K row, work 7 rows in st st.
K one row (WS).
Break off white and change to pink.
Starting with a K row, work 16 rows in st st.
Cast off.

FINISHING
**Body and head Finish as for Goldilocks (see page 96), but use lilac yarn to shape neck.
Legs Join centre back (row ends) leg seam and bottom of foot (cast-on edge), using matching yarn for each section and leaving top edge of each leg open. Turn legs RS out. Stuff each leg firmly and oversew top edge tog, keeping seam at centre back. Sew legs to lower edge of body.
Arms Finish arms as for Goldilocks, but omit wrist shaping. Do not sew arms to body until sleeves have been completed.**
Hair Loosely wrap light brown yarn about 40 times round a 7 cm (2½ in) piece of card. Slip looped yarn carefully off card, keeping it folded in half. Wrap a separate length of light brown yarn round the centre of the looped yarn, pull tightly and knot. Sew tied section to top of head so that the tie will be covered by hat and the front loops form a fringe.
  Make two more bunches of loops in the same way, but only wrapping about 20 times round card. Sew one to each side of head to form curls coming out from under hat at side of head.
***Embroidery Using a single 'ply' of red yarn, work a semi-circle in backstitch for mouth. Work a short horizontal straight st twice over same st for nose. Embroider eyes with black

yarn (see instructions given on page 10). Colour cheeks with red pencil.***

SMOCK

SKIRT

With lilac, cast on 70 sts.

Starting with a K row, work 4 rows in st st.

Next row (RS) *K1, K into front and back of next st, rep from * to end. (105 sts)

Starting with a P row, work 24 rows in st st.

K one row. Break off lilac. Change to maroon.

K one row.

Next row *P6, P into front and back of next st, rep from * to end. (120 sts)

Starting with a K row, work 5 rows in st st.

K one row (WS). Cast off.

SLEEVES (make 2)

With maroon, cast on 30 sts.

K 4 rows (garter st).

Starting with a P row, work 25 rows in st st.

Next row (RS) (K2tog) 15 times. (15 sts)

Break off yarn leaving a long loose end.

Using a blunt-ended needle, thread loose end through all 15 sts on needle, pull yarn to gather tightly, then fasten off.

FINISHING

Sleeves and arms Finish as for Goldilocks.

Skirt Join centre back seam (row ends) of skirt

JACK

SIZE As for Jill

TENSION As for Jill

DOLL

BODY AND HEAD

Work as for Jill, but use yellow for lilac.

ARMS AND LEGS

Work as for Jill.

HAIR

With dark brown, cast on 72 sts.

K one row.

MATERIALS FOR JACK

- Double knitting yarn: 50 g pink (arms, legs, head), 25 g yellow (body), 25 g black (shoes), 25 g maroon (trousers), 50 g dark blue (jacket), 20 g dark brown (hair), 25 g green (cap), plus a little red (features), and white (socks)
- Pair of 3¼ mm (old size 10) knitting needles *or size to obtain correct tension*
- Washable stuffing
- Red pencil for cheeks

---

and turn right side out. Put skirt on doll and sew in place just below sleeves and about 3 cm (1¼ in) below neck.

HAT

TO MAKE

With maroon, cast on 105 sts.

K 5 rows (garter st).

Next row (RS) *K1, K2tog, rep from * to end. (70 sts)

P one row.

Next row *K1, K into front and back of next st, rep from * to end. (105 sts)

Starting with a P row, work 23 rows in st st.

Next row (RS) *K1, K2tog, rep from * to end. (70sts)

P one row.

Next row (K2tog) 35 times. (35 sts)

P one row.

Next row K1, (K2tog) 17 times. (18 sts)

P one row.

Next row (K2tog) 9 times. (9 sts)

Break off yarn and fasten off as for sleeve.

FINISHING

Join hat seam (row ends). With maroon, work a running st between dec and inc row six rows from cast-on edge, leaving long loose ends. Pull ends to gather. Sew hat to head along gathering sts, covering ties on curls.

Next row (WS) *Insert right-hand needle knitwise into next st, wind yarn clockwise round point of needle, first finger of left hand and over point of needle again, then round finger and needle once more, draw the 3 loops on needle through, rep from * to end.

Next row K to end, treating each group of 3 loops as a single st and pulling loops down firmly. (72 sts)

Cast off.

FINISHING

Finish as for Jill from ** to **, but using yellow to shape neck.

Hair Join short ends of hair to form a crown of curls and sew cast-off edge of hair to head.

Embroidery Work features as for Jill from *** to *** (see pages 100-102).

TROUSERS

TO MAKE

The 2 legs are worked separately and then joined at the top.

First leg

*With maroon, cast on 36 sts.

K 4 rows (garter st).

Starting with a P row, work 3 rows in st st, so ending with a P row.*

Break off yarn and slip sts onto a spare needle. This completes first leg.

Second leg

Rep from * to * for second leg. Do not break off yarn.

Joining legs

With RS facing, K36 sts of second leg, then K36 sts of first leg from spare needle. (72 sts)

Starting with a P row, work 17 rows in st st, so ending with a P row.

K 3 rows (garter st).

Cast off.

FINISHING

Join centre back seam (row ends) of trousers starting at the cast-off edge and finishing at the point where the legs were joined, then join each leg seam (row ends) separately. Turn right side out.

Using a length of maroon yarn, work a running st along top of trousers just below garter st edge, leaving long loose ends.

Put trousers on doll and pull loose ends to gather to fit waist. Tie ends tog and sew trousers in place.

JACKET

MAIN PART

With dark blue, cast on 68 sts.

K 4 rows (garter st).

Next row (WS) K2, P64, K2.

**K one row.

Next row K2, P64, K2.**

Rep from ** to ** 12 times more.

Next row (K2tog) 34 times. (34 sts)

K 3 rows (garter st).

Cast off.

SLEEVES

Work two sleeves as for sleeves of Jill's smock, but use dark blue yarn.

FINISHING

Main part Sew cast-off edge of jacket to neck of doll, with centre of cast-off edge at centre back of doll.

Sleeves and arms Finish sleeves, insert arms and join to body as for Goldilocks (see instructions on page 97), sewing arms and sleeves to doll through jacket.

CAP

TO MAKE

With green, cast on 28 sts.

K one row.

P one row.

Brim shaping

***Next row** K2tog, K to last 2 sts, K2tog.

Next row P2tog, P to last 2 sts, P2tog.***

Rep from *** to *** once more. (20 sts)

Starting with a K row, work 4 rows in st st, so ending with a P row.

****Next row** (RS) K into the front and back of first st, K to last st, K into the front and back of last st.

Next row P into front and back of first st, P to last st, P into front and back of last st.****

Rep from **** to **** once more. (28 sts)

Cap shaping

Cast on 22 sts at end of last row. (50 sts)

K one row.

Cast on 22 sts at end of last row. (72 sts)

Starting with a P row, work 13 rows in st st, so ending with a P row.

Next row (RS) *K2, K2tog, rep from * to end. (54 sts)

P one row.

Next row *K1, K2tog, rep from * to end. (36 sts)

P one row.

Next row (K2tog) 18 times. (18 sts)

Break off yarn leaving a long loose end.

Using a blunt-ended needle, thread loose end through all 18 sts on needle, pull yarn to gather tightly, then fasten off.

FINISHING

Join cap seam (row ends). Fold brim of cap in half with wrong sides tog, folding along the shortest row, and stitch in place.

Sew cap to head, securing it all around head and covering cast-off edge of dark brown looped hair.

Above: *Detail of Jack's face and cap*

THE OLD WOMAN WHO LIVED IN A SHOE

★ ★

'There was an Old Woman who lived in a shoe, she had so many children, she didn't know what to do…' She is featured here with a dozen of them!

MATERIALS FOR OLD WOMAN

- Double knitting yarn: 25 g each in pink for head and hands, white for apron and legs, black for shoes, dark blue and mid-blue for skirt, light brown for hair, lime green for body and sleeves
- Small amounts of double knitting yarn in red for features, dark pink for hair bow, and dark green for buttons
- Pair of 3¼ mm (old size 10) knitting needles *or size to obtain correct tension*
- Good quality washable stuffing
- Red pencil for cheeks

OLD WOMAN

SIZE Old Woman measures approx 24 cm (9½ in) in height (including hair), when worked in recommended tension

TENSION 27 sts and 38 rows to 10 cm (4 in) measured over st st and worked on 3¼ mm needles

Check your tension before beginning and change needle size if necessary.

DOLL

LEGS, BODY AND HEAD

The 2 legs are worked separately and then joined at the top.

FIRST LEG

*With black (for shoe), cast on 21 sts.

1st row (RS) K into front and back of each st. (42 sts)

Starting with a P row, work 5 rows in st st, so ending with a P row.

Next row (RS) (K2tog) 21 times. (21 sts)

K one row.

Break off black and change to white for top of leg.

Starting with a K row, work 24 rows in st st, so ending with a P row.*

Break off yarn and slip sts onto a spare needle. This completes first leg.

SECOND LEG

Rep from * to * for second leg. Break off yarn.

JOINING LEGS

With RS facing and with lime green (body

colour), K21 sts of second leg, then K21 sts of first leg from spare needle. (42 sts)
Starting with a P row, work 23 rows in st st, so ending with a P row.

NECK SHAPING

Next row (RS) (K2tog) 21 times. (21 sts)
Break off lime green and change to pink for head.
P one row.
Next row K into front and back of each st. (42 sts)
Starting with a P row, work 23 rows more in st st, so ending with a P row.
Next row (RS) (K2tog) 21 times. (21 sts)
Next row (P2tog) 10 times, P1. (11 sts)
Break off yarn leaving a long loose end.
Using a blunt-ended needle, thread loose end through all 11 sts on needle, pull yarn to gather tightly, then fasten off.

ARMS (make 2)

With pink, cast on 8 sts.
1st row (RS) K into front and back of each st. (16 sts)
Starting with a P row, work 5 rows in st st, so ending with a P row.
Break off pink and change to lime green.
Starting with a K row, work 22 rows more in st st, so ending with a P row.
Next row (RS) (K2tog) 8 times. (8 sts)
Cast off purlwise.

KNITTED HAIR

The 2 sides of the hair are worked separately and then joined for the top of the head.

FIRST SIDE

**With light brown, cast on 20 sts.
Starting with a K row, work 12 rows in rev st st, so ending with a P row.**
Break off yarn and slip sts onto a spare needle. This completes first side.

SECOND SIDE

Rep from ** to ** for second side. Do not break off yarn.

JOINING SIDES

With WS (K side) facing, K20 sts of second side, cast on 15 sts, then K20 sts of first side from spare needle. (55 sts)
Starting with a P row, work 5 rows in rev st st, so ending with a P row.
Next row (WS) (K2tog) 27 times, K1. (28 sts)
Starting with a P row, work 5 rows in rev st st, so ending with a P row.

Next row (WS) (K2tog) 14 times. (14 sts)
P one row.

BUN SHAPING

Next row K into front and back of each st. (28 sts)
Starting with a P row, work 7 rows in rev st st, so ending with a P row.
Next row (WS) (K2tog) 14 times. (14 sts)
P one row.
Next row (K2tog) 7 times. (7 sts)
Break off yarn leaving a long loose end.
Using a blunt-ended needle, thread loose end through all 7 sts on needle, pull yarn to gather tightly, then fasten off.

FINISHING

Body, head and legs With right sides tog, join centre back seam (row ends) of body and head down to leg division, using matching yarn for each section and leaving a small opening (for turning right side out and stuffing).
Join row ends of legs and bottom of each foot. Turn right side out.
Stuff legs, body and head firmly, then sew opening tog.
To shape neck wrap a length of body colour yarn twice round the neck between the dec and inc rows. Pull yarn tightly to gather neck, knot at centre back neck and sew ends into neck.
Arms Join arm seams (row ends) and bottom of hands, keeping seam at centre and leaving top of each arm open. Turn arms right side out.
Stuff each arm firmly and sew top tog, keeping seam at centre.
With arms seams facing body, sew one arm to each side of body just below neck.
Hair With right sides (rev st st sides) tog, join centre back seam of hair. Turn right side out.
Stuff 'bun' of hair lightly. Sew hair to head all round the edge and catch bottom of bun to top of head.
Using dark pink yarn, make a twisted cord (see page 13) 24 cm (9½ in) long and tie round bottom of bun. Tie ends into a bow at front.
Embroidery Using a single 'ply' of red yarn and working in backstitch, work a semi-circle for the Old Woman's mouth.
Using a single 'ply' of red yarn, work a short horizontal straight st and work twice over same st for nose.
Using black yarn, embroider eyes (see instructions on page 13).
Colour cheeks with red pencil.

The Old Woman

CLOTHES

SKIRT

With mid-blue, cast on 80 sts.

K 3 rows (garter st).

***With dark blue, K one row and P one row.

With mid-blue, K one row and P one row.***

Rep from *** to *** 7 times more. (32 rows of st st stripes).

Break off mid-blue and continue, using dark blue only.

Next row (RS) *K1, K2tog, rep from * to last 2 sts, K2tog. (55 sts)

K one row.

Cast off.

Make the second cuff in the same way.

CUFFS (make 2)

With lime green, cast on 24 sts.

K one row.

P one row.

Cast off.

APRON

With white, cast on 30 sts.

K 2 rows (garter st).

Next row (WS) K2, P26, K2.

K one row.

Next row (WS) K2, P26, K2.

Rep last 2 rows 7 times more.

Next row *K1, K2tog, rep from * to end. (20 sts)

STRAP SHAPING

Cast on 20 sts, then K across all 40 sts.

Cast on 20 sts, then K across all 60 sts.

K one row.

Cast off.

FINISHING

Skirt Join centre back seam (row ends) of skirt. Turn right side out.

Put skirt on doll and sew in place about 4.5 cm (1¾ in) below neck.

Apron Join row ends of apron straps and sew apron in place round waist.

Cuffs With right sides together, join row ends of both cuffs.

Turn cuffs right side out and slip them onto arms cast-on edge first, so that the cast-off edge of the cuff is level with the last row of the pink hand. Sew cuff in place along cast-on edge, leaving cast-off edge loose.

Embroider four short (doubled) horizontal sts down bodice for 'buttons'.

MATERIALS FOR CHILDREN

- Double knitting yarn: 125 g in pink for heads, hands and legs, 50 g white for socks, 75 g black for shoes
- Small amounts of double knitting yarn in 11 assorted colours for clothes and six assorted colours for hair, and red for noses and mouths
- Pair of 3¼ mm (old size 10) knitting needles *or size to obtain correct tension*
- Good quality washable stuffing
- Red pencil for cheeks

CHILDREN

SIZE Children measure approx 15.5 cm (6 in) in height, when worked in recommended tension

TENSION As for Old Woman

GIRLS

LEGS, BODY AND HEAD

Make six girl dolls, each with a different body colour.

The 2 legs of each doll are worked separately and then joined at the top.

FIRST LEG

*With black (for shoe), cast on 13 sts.

1st row (RS) K into front and back of each st. (26 sts)

Starting with a P row, work 3 rows in st st, so ending with a P row.

Next row (RS) (K2tog) 13 times. (13 sts)

K one row.

Break off black and change to white for sock.

Starting with a K row, work 5 rows in st st, so ending with a K row.

K one row (WS).

Break off white and change to pink for top of leg.

Starting with a K row, work 10 rows in st st, so ending with a P row.*

Break off yarn and slip sts onto a spare needle. This completes first leg.

SECOND LEG

Rep from * to * for second leg. Break off yarn.

JOINING LEGS

With RS facing and with body colour, K13 sts of second leg, then K13 sts of first leg from spare needle. (26 sts)

Starting with a P row, work 15 rows in st st, so ending with a P row.

NECK SHAPING

Next row (RS) (K2tog) 13 times. (13 sts)

Break off body colour and change to pink for head.

P one row.

Next row K into front and back of each st. (26 sts)

Starting with a P row, work 15 rows more in st st, so ending with a P row.

Next row (RS) (K2tog) 13 times. (13 sts)

Break off yarn leaving a long loose end.

Using a blunt-ended needle, thread loose end through all 13 sts on needle, pull yarn to gather tightly, then fasten off.

ARMS

Make 2 arms for each of six dolls, using matching body colour for sleeve.

With pink, cast on 5 sts.

1st row (RS) K into front and back of each st. (10 sts)

Starting with a P row, work 3 rows in st st, so ending with a P row.

Break off pink and change to body colour for sleeve.

K 3 rows (garter st).

Starting with a P row, work 11 rows in st st, so ending with a P row.

Next row (RS) (K2tog) 5 times. (5 sts)

Cast off purlwise.

KNITTED HAIR

With desired colour, work knitted hair for one of the girl dolls.

The 2 sides of the hair are worked separately and then joined for the top of the head.

FIRST SIDE

**With hair colour, cast on 15 sts.

Starting with a K row, work 6 rows in rev st st, so ending with a P row.**

Break off yarn and slip sts onto a spare needle. This completes first side.

SECOND SIDE

Rep from ** to ** for second side. Do not break off yarn.

JOINING SIDES

With WS (K side) facing, K15 sts of second side, cast on 10 sts, then K15 sts of first side from spare needle. (40 sts)

Starting with a P row, work 3 rows in rev st st, so ending with a P row.

Next row (WS) (K2tog) 20 times. (20 sts)

Starting with a P row, work 3 rows in rev st st, so ending with a P row.

Next row (WS) (K2tog) 10 times. (10 sts)

Break off yarn leaving a long loose end.

Using a blunt-ended needle, thread loose end through all 10 sts on needle, pull yarn to gather tightly, then fasten off.

SKIRTS

Make four of the six skirts in a contrasting colour to body colour and two of the skirts in a matching colour to body colour (to form the dresses).

Left: *Detail of Girls*

With skirt colour, cast on 60 sts.

K 2 rows (garter st).

Starting with a P row, work 7 rows in st st, so ending with a P row. (If a stripe is desired after hem work first 2 rows of 7 rows in a contrasting colour.)

Next row (RS) *K1, K2tog, rep from * to end. (40 sts)

P one row.

K one row.

Cast off.

SKIRT STRAPS

Make 2 skirt straps for one doll, using same colour as skirt.

With skirt colour, cast on 20 sts.

Cast off.

HATS

Make 3 bicolour hats each with different contrasting colours.

With first hat colour, cast on 30 sts.

K one row.

**With 2nd colour, K one row and P one row.

With first colour, K one row and P one row.**

Rep from ** to ** once more.

Break off first colour and complete with 2nd colour only.

Next row (RS) (K2tog) 15 times. (15 sts)

P one row.

Break off yarn leaving a long loose end and fasten off as for hair.

FINISHING

Finish and stuff legs, body, head and arms as for Old Woman.

Hair For knitted hair, with right sides (rev st st sides) tog, join centre back seam of hair. Turn hair right side out and sew hair to head all round the edge. Make a little bow with a single strand of contrasting colour and sew to the side of the hair.

For one doll make plaited hair with a fringe. Cut thirty 21 cm (8¼ in) lengths of yarn and fifteen 26 cm (9¼ in) lengths. Fold longer lengths in half and using a matching length of yarn, tie strands tog 2.5 cm (1 in) from fold.

Sew this tied section to top of head, positioning it so that the folded loops form a fringe and the ends hang down at sides of face. Sew fringe in place. Lay 30 shorter strands over top of head so that they cover top of head, then work backstitch along centre parting of hair to hold strands in place. Plait hair, using 15 strands for each of the three sections of the plait. Tie plaits with contrasting yarn and tie ends of yarn into bows. Trim ends of plaits.

For each of two other dolls, make a 19 cm (7½ in) plait tied at each end with a bow, using six strands of yarn for each of three sections of plait. Sew centre of plait to top of head (to be covered by a hat).

For each of two remaining dolls make bunches at sides of head. Cut forty 13.5 cm (5¼ in) lengths of yarn. Lay strands over top of head so that they cover top of head, then work backstitch along centre parting of hair to hold strands in place. Tie bunches tog at side of head with contrasting yarn and tie ends of yarn into bows. On one doll with bunches sew on a few loops at centre of forehead for fringe.

Hats Join centre back seam (row ends) of hat. Turn RS out. With two contrasting colours, make a pompon (see pages 11-12) 2 cm (¾ in) in diameter for each hat and sew to top of hat.

Sew a hat to the top of the head of two dolls with plaits and of one doll with bunches (without a fringe).

Skirt Join centre back seam (row ends) of skirt. Turn right side out. Put skirt on doll and sew in place about 2.5 cm (1 in) below neck. Sew ends of straps to front and back of skirt at waist.

Embroidery Work eyes and nose as for Old Woman. Using a single 'ply' of red yarn, work V-shaped mouths.

Colour cheeks with red pencil.

Below: Detail of five Boys

BOYS

LEGS, BODY AND HEAD
Make four Boy dolls, as for Girls, each with a different body colour.

Make two more Boy dolls, as for Girls but omitting socks (and omitting K row at top of socks) and working legs above shoes in same colour as body to form an all-in-one suit.

ARMS
Make 2 arms for each of six dolls as for Girls.

KNITTED HAIR
With desired colour, work knitted hair as for Girls for five of the Boy dolls.

TROUSERS
For four dolls, make trousers in a contrasting colour to body colour.

The 2 legs of the trousers are worked separately and then joined at the top.

FIRST LEG
*With trouser colour, cast on 20 sts.
K 2 rows (garter st).
Starting with a P row, work 9 rows in st st, so ending with a P row.*
Break off yarn and slip sts onto a spare needle.

SECOND LEG
Rep from * to * for second leg. Do not break off yarn.

JOINING LEGS
With RS facing, K20 sts of second leg, then K20 sts of first leg from spare needle. (40 sts)

Starting with a P row, work 8 rows in st st, so ending with a K row.
K one row.
Cast off.

TROUSER STRAPS
Make trouser straps as for skirt straps for Girls, working 2 straps for each of two Boy dolls, using same colour as trousers.

HAT
Make one bicolour hat as for Girls.

FINISHING
Finish and stuff legs, body, head and arms as for Old Woman.
Hat Sew hat seam and make pompon as for Girls' hats.

Hair Finish knitted hair and sew to dolls as for Girls.
For hair on remaining doll, cut thirty 10 cm (4 in) lengths of yarn. Tie lengths tog at centre with a separate length of matching yarn. Sew tied section to centre of top of head and spread ends out in a circle to cover top of head. Sew hat in place over hair and then trim ends of hair strands over forehead to form fringe.
Trousers Join centre back seam (row ends) of trousers from top to point where legs were joined on. Then join each leg seam. Turn right side out.
Put trousers on dolls and sew in place round waist.
Embroidery Work features as for Girls.
On two Boy dolls with all-in-one suits, work three 'buttons' in a contrasting colour down body as for Old Woman.

Above: *Old Woman and Children*
Below: *Detail of Boy*

SEASONAL TOYS

EASTER BUNNIES

These three little bunnies make the perfect Easter present – perhaps even an acceptable alternative to what adults might consider a surfeit of chocolate eggs! They can be knitted up almost as fast as you can say 'white rabbits'.

MATERIALS FOR EASTER BUNNIES
- Double knitting yarn: 100 g white for bunnies, 25 g pink for ears, 25 g yellow for dress
- Small amounts of double knitting yarn in green for jacket, red for dungarees and features, blue and purple for trim and black for eyes
- Pair of 3¼ mm (old size 10) knitting needles *or size to obtain correct tension*
- Good quality washable stuffing
- Red pencil for cheeks

SIZE Mr and Mrs Bunny each measure approx 18 cm (7 in) in height and Baby Bunny measures approx 13 cm (5 in) in height (including ears), when worked in recommended tension

TENSION 27 sts and 38 rows to 10 cm (4 in) measured over st st and worked on 3¼ mm needles
Check your tension before beginning and change needle size if necessary.

MR BUNNY

BODY AND HEAD
Work body and head for Mr Bunny as for Daddy and Mummy Bear (see page 98), but use white instead of light brown.

ARMS
Work arms as for Daddy and Mummy Bear, but use white instead of light brown.

LEGS (make 2)
With white, cast on 10 sts.
Starting with a K row, work 10 rows in st st, so ending with a P row.
Next row (RS) (K2tog) 5 times. (5 sts)
P one row.
Next row K into front and back of each st. (10 sts)
Starting with a P row, work 10 rows in st st, so ending with a K row.
Cast off purlwise.

EARS (make 2)
With white, cast on 14 sts.
Starting with a K row, work 20 rows in st st, so ending with a P row.
Next row (RS) (K2tog) twice, K6, (K2tog) twice. (10 sts)
P one row.

Break off white and change to pink.
With pink and starting with a K row, work 18 rows in st st.
Cast off.

JACKET
With green, cast on 50 sts.
K 2 rows (garter st).
Next row (WS) K2, P46, K2.
K one row.
Next row K2, P46, K2.
RIGHT FRONT
Next row K10, turn leaving rem 40 sts on a st holder.
Working on these 10 sts only, continue as follows:
Next row P8, K2.
Next row K to end.
Rep last 2 rows 8 times more.
Next row (WS) (K2tog) 4 times, K2. (6 sts)
Do not break off yarn, but slip sts onto a st holder.
BACK
Return to rem 40 sts on st holder and with RS facing, rejoin a separate length of green yarn and K30, then slip rem 10 sts onto a st holder.
Working on these 30 sts only, continue as follows:
Next row P to end.
Next row K to end.
Rep last 2 rows 8 times more.
Next row (WS) (K2tog) 15 times. (15 sts)
Break off yarn and slip sts onto a st holder.
LEFT FRONT
Return to rem unworked 10 sts on st holder and with RS facing, rejoin yarn and K to end.
Next row K2, P8.
Next row K to end.
Rep last 2 rows 8 times more.
Next row (WS) K2, (K2tog) 4 times. (6 sts)
Slip sts onto a st holder.

NECKBAND

Now with RS facing, cast off 6 sts on first st
   holder (right front), continue across sts on
   next st holder and cast off 15 sts, then cast off
   6 sts on last st holder (left front).

FINISHING

Finish body and head and arms and legs as for
Daddy and Mummy Bear (see page 98), but use
white to shape neck. Sew arms and legs to
body as shown.

Ears Fold one ear in half with RS of pink half
facing RS of white half. Join side seam (row
ends) on first side of ear and when top of ear is
reached, secure yarn but do not break off. Now
work a running st along fold, pull yarn to gather
top of ear slightly and secure yarn, then
continue seam down other side of ear joining
row ends and leaving lower edge open. Do not
break off yarn. Turn ear right side out.

   Secure yarn, then with WS of white side of ear
facing WS of pink side of ear, work a running st
through both layers along lower edge, pull yarn to
gather bottom of ear tightly and fasten off yarn.

   Sew other ear tog in same way.

   Sew ears to top of head, with pink sides
facing front.

Jacket Put jacket on bunny and sew cast-off
edge of jacket to neck. Using blue yarn, make a
bow and sew to centre front neck.

Tail For tail make a pompon (see pages 11-12)
4 cm (1½ in) in diameter and sew to back of
bunny, stitching through jacket.

Embroidery Using a single 'ply' of red yarn and
working in satin st, make a triangle (with one
corner facing downwards) for nose. Then still
using red, work a vertical straight st from centre
of tip of nose to centre of mouth. Work an
upside down V-shape for mouth.

   Using black yarn, embroider eyes (see instructions on page 10).

   Colour cheeks with red pencil.

MRS BUNNY
. . . .

BODY AND HEAD

Work body and head for Mrs Bunny as for
   Daddy and Mummy Bear (see page 98), but
   use white instead of light brown.

ARMS

Work arms as for Daddy and Mummy Bear, but
   use white instead of light brown.

LEGS AND EARS

Work as for Mr Bunny.

DRESS

With yellow, cast on 75 sts.
K 2 rows (garter st).
Starting with a P row, work 11 rows in st st, so
   ending with a P row.
Next row (RS) *K1, K2tog, rep from * to end.
   (50 sts)
Starting with a P row, work 7 rows in st st, so
   ending with a P row.
Next row (RS) (P2tog) 25 times. (25 sts)
Cast off knitwise.

SLEEVES (make 2)

With yellow, cast on 24 sts.
K one row.

Next row (RS) K into front and back of each st.
   (48 sts)
Starting with a P row, work 5 rows in st st.
Next row (RS) (K2tog) 24 times. (24 sts)
P one row.
Next row (K2tog) 12 times. (12 sts)
P one row.
Next row (K2tog) 6 times. (6 sts)
Break off yarn leaving a long loose end.
Using a blunt-ended needle, thread loose end
   through all 6 sts on needle, pull yarn to gather
   tightly, then fasten off.

FINISHING

Finish bunny as for Mr Bunny, but do not sew
on arms until dress has been completed.
Dress Put dress on bunny and join centre back
seam (row ends) of dress while it is on bunny.

   Join sleeve seams (row ends). Turn right side
out. Insert top of arms into sleeves with seams
lined up, then sew tops of arms to sleeves.
With sleeve seams facing body, sew one sleeve
to each side of body just below neck.

   Using purple yarn, work four chain sts radiating
out from same centre for detail at front of dress.
Tail Make tail as for Mr Bunny and sew to back
of bunny, stitching through dress.
Embroidery Work features as for Mr Bunny and
colour cheeks with red pencil.

BABY BUNNY

BODY AND HEAD

Work as for Baby Bear (see page 98), but use white instead of light brown.

ARMS

Work arms as for Baby Bear, but use white instead of light brown.

LEGS (make 2)

With white, cast on 7 sts.

Starting with a K row, work 6 rows in st st, so ending with a P row.

Next row (RS) (K2tog) 3 times, K1. (4 sts)

P one row.

Next row (K into front and back of next st) 3 times, K1. (7 sts)

Starting with a P row, work 6 rows in st st, so ending with a K row. Cast off purlwise.

EARS (make 2)

With white, cast on 10 sts.

Starting with a K row, work 14 rows in st st, so ending with a P row.

Next row (RS) (K2tog) twice, K2, (K2tog) twice. (6 sts)

P one row.

Break off white and change to pink.

Starting with a K row, work 12 rows in st st. Cast off.

DUNGAREES

With red, cast on 18 sts.

1st row (RS) K into front and back of each st. (36 sts)

Starting with a P row, work 9 rows in st st, so ending with a P row.

BIB SHAPING

Next row (RS) Cast off 13 sts, K10 (including st already on needle after cast off), cast off last 13 sts.

With WS facing, rejoin yarn to 10 sts left on needle and continue as follows:

Next row K1, P8, K1.

Next row K to end.

Next row K1, P8, K1.

Rep last 2 rows once more.

Cast off knitwise.

STRAPS (make 2)

With red, cast on 14 sts.

Cast off.

FINISHING

Finish bunny as for Mr Bunny, but do not sew on legs until dungarees have been completed.

Dungarees Join centre back seam (row ends) of dungarees, then oversew cast-on edge every alternate st, pull yarn to gather tightly and fasten off. Turn right side out.

Put dungarees on bunny and sew one end of each strap to corner of bib. Take straps over shoulders and join ends to dungarees at either side of centre back seam. Sew legs to bottom of dungarees.

Tail For tail make a pompon (see pages 11-12) 2.5 cm (1 in) in diameter and sew to back of bunny, stitching through dungarees.

Embroidery Work features as for Mr Bunny and colour cheeks with red pencil.

Below: *Mrs Bunny and Baby Bunny*

BEACH BABIES

On summer days thoughts turn to sun, sea and sand, with Milly Mermaid and her friends, the multi-legged Octopus Family.

MATERIALS FOR MILLY MERMAID

- Double knitting yarn: 40 g pink for body, head and arms, 25 g green for tail, 25 g yellow for hair
- Small amounts of double knitting yarn in black for eyes, red for nose and mouth, blue for hair bow
- Pair of 3¼ mm (old size 10) knitting needles *or size to obtain correct tension*
- Good quality washable stuffing
- Red pencil for cheeks

MILLY MERMAID

SIZE Milly Mermaid measures approx 24 cm (9½ in) in length, when worked in recommended tension

TENSION 27 sts and 38 rows to 10 cm (4 in) measured over st st and worked on 3¼ mm needles
Check your tension before beginning and change needle size if necessary.

BODY AND HEAD
With green, cast on 2 sts.
K one row.
P one row.
Next row (RS) K into front and back of each st. (4 sts)
P one row.
*****Next row** K into front and back of first st, K to last st, K into front and back of last st.
P one row.*
Rep from * to * 17 times more, so ending with a P (WS) row. (40 sts)
P one row (RS).
Break off green and change to pink for top body and head.
Starting with a P row, work 13 rows in st st, so ending with a P row.
NECK SHAPING
Next row (RS) (K2tog) 20 times. (20 sts)
P one row.
Next row K into front and back of each st. (40 sts)
Starting with a P row, work 19 rows in st st, so ending with a P row.
Next row (RS) (K2tog) 20 times. (20 sts)
P one row.
Next row (K2tog) 10 times. (10 sts)
Break off yarn leaving a long loose end.
Using a blunt-ended needle, thread loose end

through all 10 sts on needle, pull yarn to gather
  tightly, then fasten off.

ARMS (make 2)
With pink, cast on 14 sts.
Starting with a K row, work 24 rows in st st, so
  ending with a P row.
Next row (RS) (K2tog) 7 times. (7 sts)
Break off yarn leaving a long loose end and
  fasten off as for top of head.

TAIL (make 2)
With green, cast on 7 sts.
1st row (RS) K into front and back of each st.
  (14 sts)

Starting with a P row, work 11 rows in st st, so
  ending with a P row.
Next row (RS) (K2tog) 7 times. (7 sts)
Break off yarn leaving a long loose end and
  fasten off as for top of head.

FINISHING
Body and head Join centre back seam (row
ends) of body and head, leaving opening in
head seam. Turn body and head right side out.
  Stuff body and head firmly. Then join head
seam opening.
  To shape neck wrap a length of pink yarn
twice round the neck between the dec and inc
rows. Pull yarn tightly to gather neck, knot at
centre back neck and sew ends into neck.
Arms Join arm seams (row ends), leaving top of
each arm (cast-on edge) open. Turn arms right
side out.
  Stuff each arm firmly and oversew cast-on
edge tog, keeping seam at centre.
  To shape wrist wrap a length of pink yarn
once round arm about nine rows from gathered
end. Pull yarn tightly to gather wrist, knot at
seam and sew ends into seam.
  With seams facing body sew one arm to each
side of body just below neck.
Tail Join row ends of each tail piece, leaving
cast-on edge open and turn right side out. Do
not stuff. Oversew cast-on edge tog, keeping
seam at side and sew one tail piece to each
side of tip of body.
Hair Cut fifty 25 cm (10 in) lengths and sixty
36 cm (14 in) lengths of yellow hair. Holding
shorter lengths tog, wrap a separate length of
yellow yarn round centre and tie. Sew the tied
section to the top of the head so that the cut
ends hang down over sides of head. Then holding the longer lengths tog, fold in half and tie
4 cm (1½ in) from folded end. Sew to top of
head so that folded end forms fringe and cut
ends hang down over back of head.
  Using blue yarn, make a twisted cord 17 cm
(6½ in) long (see page 13) and tie into a bow.
Sew bow to top of head.
Embroidery Using a single 'ply' of red yarn,
work a V-shaped mouth.
  Using a single 'ply' of red yarn, work a short
horizontal straight st and work twice over same
st for nose.
  Using black yarn, embroider eyes (see instructions on page 10).
  Colour cheeks with red pencil.

*Daddy Octopus and
Milly Mermaid*

MATERIALS FOR DADDY OCTOPUS

- Double knitting yarn: 125 g light green for body, 25 g black for hat, 50 g green for shoes
- Small amounts of double knitting yarn in purple for bow tie and red for nose and mouth
- Pair of 3¼ mm (old size 10) knitting needles *or size to obtain correct tension*
- Good quality washable stuffing
- Piece of plastic (see Finishing)

DADDY OCTOPUS

SIZE Daddy Octopus measures approx 35 cm (13¾ in) in diameter, when worked in recommended tension

TENSION 27 sts and 38 rows to 10 cm (4 in) measured over st st and worked on 3¼ mm needles
Check your tension before beginning and change needle size if necessary.

BODY

With light green, cast on 20 sts.
1st row (RS) K into front and back of each st. (40 sts)
P one row.
Next row K into front and back of each st. (80 sts)
Starting with a P row, work 40 rows in st st, so ending with a K row.
Next row (WS) (P2tog) 40 times. (40 sts)
Next row (K2tog) 20 times. (20 sts)
Next row (P2tog) 10 times. (10 sts)
Break off yarn leaving a long loose end.
Using a blunt-ended needle, thread loose end through all 10 sts on needle, pull yarn to gather tightly, then fasten off.

LEGS (make 8)

With green, cast on 18 sts.
1st row (RS) K into front and back of each st. (36 sts)
Starting with a P row, work 9 rows in st st.
Next row (RS) K6, (K3tog) 8 times, K6. (20 sts)
K one row.
P one row.
Break off green and change to light green.
Starting with a P row, work 45 rows in st st. Cast off.

HAT

With black, cast on 8 sts.
K one row.
Next row K into front and back of each st. (16 sts)
K 3 rows.
Next row K into front and back of each st. (32 sts)
K 5 rows.
Next row K into front and back of each st. (64 sts)

K 3 rows.
Starting with a K row, work 4 rows in st st, so ending with a P row.
Make ridge on next row as follows:
Next row K tog first st on needle with first st from first row of st st, *K next st on needle with next st from first row of st st, rep from * to end. (64 sts)
K 9 rows.

BRIM SHAPING
Begin brim on next row as follows:
Next row *K1, K into front and back of next st, rep from * to end. (96 sts)
K 7 rows. Cast off loosely.

FINISHING

Body Join centre back seam (row ends) of body, leaving cast-on edge open. Turn right side out.
Stuff body firmly. Oversew cast-on edge every alternate st, pull yarn to gather tightly and fasten off.
Legs Join bottom of foot and row ends of each leg, leaving cast-off edge open. Turn legs right side out.
Stuff each leg firmly and oversew top edge tog, keeping seam at centre.
With seam facing downwards, sew each leg to bottom of body about 2 cm (¾ in) from the centre.***
Hat Join hat seam (row ends), then oversew the cast-on edge every alternate st, pull yarn to gather tightly and fasten off. Turn hat RS out.
Work running st round hat at bottom of crown (beginning of brim), pull yarn to gather slightly and fasten off.
Using a soft plastic ice cream lid, cut a plastic circle 8 cm (3 in) in diameter and place inside top of hat.
Stuff hat lightly and sew hat to top of head, stitching along gathered row.
Hair Using green yarn, sew a few loops coming out from underneath the hat at centre of forehead for the hair.
Bow tie Using purple yarn, make a twisted cord 20.5 cm (8 in) long (see page 13). Tie in a bow and sew to centre front neck.
Embroidery Using a single 'ply' of red yarn, work a semi-circle in backstitch for the mouth.
Using a whole strand of red yarn, work a short horizontal straight st and work twice over the same st for nose.
Using black yarn, embroider eyes (see the instructions on page 10).

MATERIALS FOR MUMMY OCTOPUS

- Double knitting yarn: 125 g light green for body, 25 g beige for hat, 50 g blue for shoes, 25 g green for hair
- Small amounts of double knitting yarn in yellow, red and pink for flowers and black for eyes
- Pair of 3¼ mm (old size 10) knitting needles *or size to obtain correct tension*
- Good quality washable stuffing

MATERIALS FOR BOY OCTOPUS

- Double knitting yarn: 60 g light green for body, 25 g yellow for hat, 25 g maroon for hat, 25 g blue for shoes, 25 g white for socks
- Small amounts of double knitting yarn in green for hair, black for eyes and red for mouth and nose
- Pair of 3¼ mm (old size 10) knitting needles *or size to obtain correct tension*
- Good quality washable stuffing

MUMMY OCTOPUS

SIZE As for Daddy Octopus

TENSION As for Daddy Octopus

BODY AND LEGS
Work as for Daddy Octopus, but use blue instead of green for shoes.

HAT
Work as for Daddy Octopus, but use beige instead of black.

HAT RIBBON
With blue, cast on 85 sts.
K 3 rows. Cast off.

LEAVES (make 3)
With green, cast on 8 sts.
Cast off.

FLOWERS (make 3)
With yellow, cast on 5 sts.
1st row K into front and back of each st. (10 sts)
Cast off loosely.

BOY OCTOPUS

SIZE Boy Octopus measures approx 25.5 cm (10 in) in diameter, when worked in recommended tension

TENSION As for Daddy Octopus

BODY
With light green, cast on 15 sts.
1st row (RS) K into front and back of each st. (30 sts)
P one row.
Next row K into front and back of each st. (60 sts)
Starting with a P row, work 30 rows in st st, so ending with a K row.
Next row (WS) (P2tog) 30 times. (30 sts)
Next row (K2tog) 15 times. (15 sts)
Next row (P2tog) 7 times, P1. (8 sts)
Break off yarn leaving a long loose end.
Using a blunt-ended needle, thread loose end through all 8 sts on needle, pull yarn to gather tightly, then fasten off.

Make 2 more flowers, one with red and one with pink.

FINISHING
Finish as for Daddy Octopus to ***.
   Hair Cut twelve 17 cm (6½ in) lengths of green yarn for hair. Tie one end, then beginning at this end, divide lengths into three groups of four strands each and plait yarn. Tie other end. Fold plait in half and sew ends of plait to top of head so that bottom loop is half way down body.
   Make 11 more plaits in same way and sew round top of head.
Hat Finish hat as for Daddy Octopus. Then join row ends of hat ribbon and sew to base of crown of hat.
   Join row ends of flowers. Sew leaves and flowers in a little group to side of hat on top of hat ribbon, working black French knots for the centres of flowers.
   Sew hat to top of head.
   Using green yarn, sew a few loops coming out from under hat at centre of forehead to form the fringe.
Embroidery Embroider facial features as for Daddy Octopus on previous page.

LEGS (make 8)
With blue, cast on 12 sts.
1st row (RS) K into front and back of each st. (24 sts)
Starting with a P row, work 5 rows in st st, so ending with a P row.
Next row (RS) K4, (K3tog) 5 times, K5. (14 sts)
P 2 rows.
Break off blue and change to white for socks.
Starting with a P row, work 10 rows in st st, so ending with a K row.
Break off white and change to light green.
Starting with a P row, work 20 rows in st st, so ending with a K row.
Cast off purlwise.

SOCK TOPS (make 8)
With white, cast on 25 sts.
1st rib row (RS) K1, *P1, K1, rep from * to end.
2nd rib row P1, *K1, P1, rep from * to end.
Cast off in rib.

HAT
With maroon, cast on 70 sts.

1st rib row (RS) *K1, P1, rep from * to end.
Rep last row 3 times more.
**With maroon, K one row and P one row.
With yellow, K one row and P one row.**
Rep from ** to ** twice more.
Next row With maroon, *K3, K2tog, rep from *
   to end. (56 sts)
Next row With maroon, P to end.
Next row With yellow, *K2, K2tog, rep from *
   to end. (42 sts)
Next row With yellow, P to end.
Next row With maroon, *K1, K2tog, rep from *
   to end. (28 sts)
Next row With maroon, P to end.
Break off maroon.
Next row With yellow, (K2tog) 14 times.
   (14 sts)
Break off yarn leaving a long loose end and
   fasten off as for body.

FINISHING
Finish as for Daddy Octopus to ***.
Sock tops Join row ends of each sock top. Slip
sock tops onto legs and join cast-on edge of
top to last row of white, with cast-off edge of
sock top facing shoe.****
Hat Join hat seam (row ends) and turn right side
out. Turn up rib of hat for brim.
   Make a pompon (see instructions on pages
11-12) 3 cm (1¼ in) in diameter and sew to the
centre top of hat.
   Sew hat to top of head.
Hair Using green yarn, sew a few loops coming
out from under hat at centre of forehead to form
the hair.
Embroidery Embroider the mouth and eyes as
for Daddy Octopus. Using a single 'ply' of red
yarn, work a short horizontal straight st and
work twice over same st to make the nose.

Below: *Boy Octopus
and Mummy Octopus*

MATERIALS FOR GIRL OCTOPUS

· Double knitting yarn:
  60 g light green for
  body, 25 g pink for
  hat, 25 g dusty pink
  for shoes, 25 g white
  for socks
· Small amounts of
  double knitting yarn in
  green for hair,
  yellow for bows, black
  for eyes and red for
  mouth and nose
· Pair of 3¼ mm (old
  size 10) knitting
  needles *or size to
  obtain correct tension*
· Good quality washable
  stuffing

GIRL OCTOPUS

SIZE As for Boy Octopus

TENSION As for Daddy Octopus

BODY AND LEGS
Work as for Boy Octopus, but use dusty pink instead of blue for shoes.

HAT
With pink, cast on 105 sts.
K 3 rows (garter st).
Next row (RS) *K1, K2tog, rep from * to end. (70 sts)
Starting with a P row, work 13 rows in st st, so ending with a P row.
Next row (RS) *K3, K2tog, rep from * to end. (56 sts)
P one row.
Next row *K2, K2tog, rep from * to end. (42 sts)
P one row.
Next row *K1, K2tog, rep from * to end. (28 sts)

P one row.
Next row (K2tog) 14 times. (14 sts)
Break off yarn leaving a long loose end and fasten off as for body.

FINISHING
Finish as for Boy Octopus to ****.
Hair Using yellow yarn, make two twisted cords each 15 cm (6 in) long (see instructions for making a twisted cord on page 13). Then cut eighteen 28 cm (11 in) lengths of green yarn for the hair.
  Tie one yellow cord in a bow around green lengths 2 cm (¾ in) from one end. Then beginning as this end, divide lengths into three groups of six strands each and plait yarn. Tie other end with remaining yellow cord.
  Sew middle of plait to top of head. Trim the ends of the plait.
Hat Join hat seam (row ends) and turn right side out. Sew hat to top of head.
Embroidery Embroider mouth and eyes as for Daddy Octopus. Using a single 'ply' of red yarn, work a short horizontal straight st and work twice over same st for nose.

MATERIALS FOR BABY OCTOPUS

- Double knitting yarn: 30 g light green for body and small amounts in green for hair, black for eyes and red for mouth and nose
- Pair of 3¼ mm (old size 10) knitting needles *or size to obtain correct tension*
- Good quality washable stuffing

BABY OCTOPUS

SIZE Baby Octopus measures approx 18 cm (7 in) in diameter, when worked in recommended tension

TENSION As for Daddy Octopus

BODY
With light green, cast on 10 sts.
1st row (RS) K into front and back of each st. (20 sts)
P one row.
Next row K into front and back of each st. (40 sts)
Starting with a P row, work 20 rows in st st, so ending with a K row.
Next row (WS) (P2tog) 20 times. (20 sts)
Next row (K2tog) 10 times. (10 sts)
Next row (P2tog) 5 times. (5 sts)
Break off yarn leaving a long loose end.
Using a blunt-ended needle, thread loose end through all 5 sts on needle, pull yarn to gather tightly, then fasten off.

LEGS (make 8)
With light green, cast on 9 sts.
1st row (RS) K into front and back of each st. (18 sts)

Starting with a P row, work 5 rows in st st, so ending with a P row.
Next row (RS) K3, (K3tog) 4 times, K3. (10 sts)
Starting with a P row, work 20 rows in st st, so ending with a K row.
Cast off purlwise.

FINISHING
Body With wrong sides tog, join centre back seam (row ends) of body, leaving cast-on edge open. Stuff body firmly. Oversew cast-on edge every alternate st, pull yarn to gather tightly and fasten off.
Legs With wrong sides tog, join bottom of foot and row ends of each leg, leaving cast-off edge open.
   Stuff each leg firmly and oversew top edge tog, keeping seam at centre. With seam facing downwards, sew each leg to bottom of body about 1.5 cm (½ in) from centre.
Hair Cut sixteen 3 cm (1¼ in) lengths of green yarn. Holding lengths tog, wrap a separate length of green yarn round centre and tie. Sew tied section to centre of top of head and spread out in a circle.
Embroidery Embroider mouth and eyes as for Daddy Octopus. Using a single 'ply' of red yarn, work a short horizontal straight st and work twice over same st for nose.

HALLOWEEN WITCH

'Up, up and away!' cackled Wendy Witch as she flew through the air on a magic broomstick, accompanied by her lucky black Cat and plump yellow Pumpkin.

MATERIALS FOR WENDY WITCH

- Double knitting yarn: 75 g pink for hands, legs and head, 100 g light green for body and dress, 25 g green for dress, 75 g black for shoes, cape and hat, 20 g red for hair
- Pair of 3¼ mm (old size 10) knitting needles *or size to obtain correct tension*
- Good quality washable stuffing
- Red pencil for cheeks

WENDY WITCH

SIZE Wendy Witch measures approx 37.5 cm (14¾ in) in height (including hat), when worked in recommended tension

TENSION 27 sts and 38 rows to 10 cm (4 in) measured over st st and worked on 3¼ mm needles
   Check your tension before beginning and change needle size if necessary.

DOLL

LEGS, BODY AND HEAD
The 2 legs are worked separately and then joined at the top.
RIGHT LEG
*With black (for shoes), cast on 24 sts.
1st row (RS) K into front and back of each st. (48 sts)
Starting with a P row, work 13 rows in st st, so ending with a P row.*
Next row (RS) K6, (K3tog) 9 times, K15. (30 sts)
**Starting with a P row, work 5 rows in st st, so ending with a P row.
Break off black and change to pink.
Starting with a K row, work 26 rows in st st, so ending with a P row.**
Break off yarn and slip sts onto a spare needle. This completes right leg.
LEFT LEG
Work as for right leg from * to *.
Next row (RS) K15, (K3tog) 9 times, K6. (30 sts)
Complete as for right leg from ** to **.
Break off yarn.
JOINING LEGS
With RS facing and with light green (body colour), K30 sts of left leg, then K30 sts of right leg from spare needle. (60 sts)

Starting with a P row, work 31 rows in st st, so ending with a P row.

NECK SHAPING

Next row (RS) (K2tog) 30 times. (30 sts)

Break off light green and change to pink.

P one row.

Next row K into front and back of each st. (60 sts)

Starting with a P row, work 29 rows in st st.

Wendy Witch

Next row (RS) (K2tog) 30 times. (30 sts)

Next row (P2tog) 15 times. (15 sts)

Break off yarn leaving a long loose end.

Using a blunt-ended needle, thread loose end through all 15 sts on needle, pull yarn to gather tightly, then fasten off.

ARMS (make 2)

With light green, cast on 12 sts.

Starting with a K row, work 2 rows in st st, so ending with a P row.

*****Next row** (RS) K into front and back of first st, K to last st, K into front and back of last st.

P one row.*

Rep from * to * 6 times more. (26 sts)

Starting with a K row, work 12 rows in st st, so ending with a P row.

Break off light green and change to pink for hand.

Starting with a K row, work 10 rows more in st st, so ending with a P row.

Next row (RS) (K2tog) 13 times. (13 sts)

Break off yarn leaving a long loose end and fasten off as for top of head.

NOSE

With pink, cast on 8 sts.

Starting with a K row, work 6 rows in st st, so ending with a P row.

Next row (RS) K2tog, K4, K2tog. (6 sts)

P one row.

Next row K2tog, K2, K2tog. (4 sts)

P one row.

Next row (K2tog) twice. (2 sts)

Next row P2tog. Fasten off.

FINISHING

Finish and stuff body, head and legs as for Old Woman in Shoe (see page 106).

Arms Join arm seams (row ends) up to top shaping. Turn arms right side out.

Stuff each arm firmly and sew cast-on edge and shaped edges of one arm to each side of body between neck and waist 6 cm (2¼ in) below neck.

Hair Cut ninety 30 cm (12 in) lengths of red yarn and holding lengths tog, wrap a separate length of red yarn round centre and tie.

Sew the tied section to the top of the head and spread ends out to cover the back and sides of head. (When the hat is sewn on it will keep hair in place.)

Nose Join nose seam (row ends) with wrong

sides tog and stuff firmly. Sew nose to head about 3.5 cm (1¼ in) up from neck.

Embroidery Using a single 'ply' of red yarn, work an upside down V-shape for mouth.

Using black yarn, embroider eyes (see instructions on page 10).

Using a single 'ply' of black yarn work a short slanted st for each eyebrow.

Colour cheeks and nose with red pencil.

DRESS

SKIRT

With green, cast on 112 sts.

K 3 rows (garter st).

**With light green and starting with a K row, work 4 rows in st st.

With green and starting with a K row, work 4 rows more in st st.**

Rep from ** to ** once more.

Break off green and complete with light green.

Starting with a K row, work 26 rows in st st, so ending with a P row.

Next row (RS) *K3, K2tog, rep from * to last 2 sts, K2. (90 sts)

P one row.

Cast off.

CUFFS (make 2)

With green, cast on 35 sts.

K 3 rows (garter st).

Cast off.

FINISHING

Skirt Join centre back seam (row ends) of skirt. Turn right side out.

Put skirt on doll and sew cast-off edge to waist about 6 cm (2¼ in) below neck.

Cuffs Join row ends of cuffs. Slip cuffs onto arms and position so that cuff overlaps hand and sleeve. Sew each cuff in place round sleeve, leaving edge round hand loose.

CAPE

TO MAKE

With black, cast on 84 sts.

K 4 rows (garter st).

Next row (WS) K3, P78, K3.

*K one row.

Next row K3, P78, K3.*

Rep from * to * 18 times more.

Next row (K2tog) 42 times. (42 sts)

K one row.

Cast off.

FINISHING

Using black yarn, make two twisted cords each 15 cm (6 in) long (see page 13). Then sew one cord to each corner of cape at cast-off edge.

Put cape on doll and tie twisted cords in a bow at front neck.

HAT

TO MAKE

With black, cast on 121 sts loosely.

K 7 rows (garter st).

Next row (RS) *K1, K2tog, rep from * to last st, K1. (81 sts)

Starting with a P row, work 4 rows in st st, so ending with a K row.

Next row (WS) *P7, P2tog, rep from * to end. (72 sts)

Starting with a K row, work 4 rows in st st, so ending with a P row.

Next row (RS) *K6, K2tog, rep from * to end. (63 sts)

Starting with a P row, work 4 rows in st st.

Next row *P5, P2tog, rep from * to end. (54 sts)

Starting with a K row, work 4 rows in st st.

Next row *K4, K2tog, rep from * to end. (45 sts)

Starting with a P row, work 4 rows in st st.

Next row *P3, P2tog, rep from * to end. (36 sts)

Starting with a K row, work 4 rows in st st.

Next row *K2, K2tog, rep from * to end. (27 sts)

Starting with a P row, work 4 rows in st st.

Next row *P1, P2tog, rep from * to end. (18 sts)

Starting with a K row, work 4 rows in st st.

Next row (K2tog) 9 times. (9 sts)

Break off yarn leaving a long loose end.

Using a blunt-ended needle, thread loose end through all 9 sts on needle, pull yarn to gather tightly, then fasten off.

FINISHING

With right sides tog, join hat seam (row ends). Then turn hat right side out. Stuff hat lightly and sew to top of head along first row of st st. Trim ends of red hair.

MATERIALS FOR PUMPKIN AND CAT

- Double knitting yarn: 25 g black for cat and 10 g yellow-orange for pumpkin
- Small amounts of double knitting yarn in green and pink
- Pair of 3¼ mm (old size 10) knitting needles *or size to obtain correct tension*
- Good quality washable stuffing

PUMPKIN AND CAT

SIZE The Pumpkin measures approx 7 cm (2¾ in) in diameter and 5 cm (2 in) in height. The Cat measures approx 10 cm (4 in) in height (including ears), when worked in recommended tension

TENSION As for Wendy Witch

PUMPKIN

TO MAKE
With yellow-orange, cast on 25 sts.
1st row (RS) K into front and back of each st. (50 sts)
Starting with a P row, work 23 rows in st st, so ending with a P row.
Next row (RS) (K2tog) 25 times. (25 sts)
Next row (P2tog) 12 times, P1. (13 sts)
Break off yarn leaving a long loose end.
Using a blunt-ended needle, thread loose end through all 13 sts on needle, pull yarn to gather tightly, then fasten off.

LEAVES (make 3)
With green, cast on 3 sts.
1st row K into front and back of first st, then K to end.
Rep first row once more. (5 sts)
K 4 rows (garter st).
Next row K2tog, K to end.
Rep last row once more. (3 sts)
K 3 rows.
Cast off.

STALK
With green, cast on 7 sts.
K 6 rows (garter st). Cast off.

FINISHING
Join pumpkin seam (row ends), leaving cast-on edge open. Turn right side out and stuff firmly. Oversew cast-on edge every alternate st, pull yarn to gather tightly and fasten off.

To shape pumpkin, secure a length of yellow-orange yarn to centre top and pass needle from centre top to centre bottom, then back up to top. Pull yarn tightly to make indents at top and bottom, then fasten off yarn.
Leaves and stalk Sew cast-off end of each leaf to centre top. Join cast-off edge of stalk to cast-on edge, pulling slightly to curve stalk. Sew one end of stalk to centre top of pumpkin on top of leaves.
Embroidery Using a single 'ply' of black yarn and working in satin stitch, make two triangles for eyes. Still using black, work a short doubled horizontal straight st for nose. Then work a zigzag mouth.

CAT

BODY AND HEAD
With black, cast on 16 sts.
1st row (RS) K into front and back of each st. (32 sts)
Starting with a P row, work 15 rows in st st for body, so ending with a P row.
NECK SHAPING
Next row (RS) (K2tog) 16 times. (16 sts)
P one row.
Next row K into front and back of each st. (32 sts)
Starting with a P row, work 13 rows in st st for head, so ending with a P row.
Next row (RS) (K2tog) 16 times. (16 sts)
Next row (P2tog) 8 times. (8 sts)
Break off yarn leaving a long loose end.
Using a blunt-ended needle, thread loose end through all 8 sts on needle, pull yarn to gather tightly, then fasten off.

FEET (make 2)
With black, cast on 6 sts.
1st row (RS) K into front and back of each st. (12 sts)
Starting with a P row, work 7 rows in st st, so ending with a P row.
Next row (RS) (K2tog) 6 times. (6 sts)
Break off yarn leaving a long loose end and fasten off as for top of head.

EARS (make 2)
With black, cast on 10 sts.
Starting with a K row, work 10 rows in st st.
Cast off.

TAIL
With black, cast on 8 sts.
Starting with a K row, work 22 rows in st st, so ending with a P row.
Next row (RS) (K2tog) 4 times. (4 sts)
Break off yarn leaving a long loose end and fasten off as for top of head.

FINISHING

Body and head Join centre back seam (row ends) of body and head, leaving cast-on edge open. Turn right side out.

Stuff body and head firmly. Oversew cast-on edge every alternate st, pull yarn to gather tightly and fasten off.

To shape neck wrap a length of black yarn twice round neck between the dec and inc rows. Pull yarn tightly to gather neck, knot at centre back neck and sew ends into neck.

Feet With wrong sides tog, join row ends of each foot, leaving cast-on edge open. Stuff each foot firmly. Oversew cast-on edge every alternate st, pull yarn to gather tightly and fasten off. When feet are completed, sew to lower front of body with seam facing body.

Ears Fold ears in half diagonally with wrong sides tog and join sides. Sew diagonal edge of each ear to top of head.

Tail With wrong sides tog, join row ends of tail, leaving cast-on edge open. Stuff tail firmly and oversew cast-on edge tog. Sew tail to back of cat. Work a running st from end to end of tail, pull to curve tail and fasten off.

Embroidery Using a single 'ply' of pink yarn and working in satin st, work a triangle for nose. Still using pink, work a short vertical straight st from centre of nose to centre of mouth. Work a V-shaped mouth.

Using green or white yarn, embroider eyes horizontally (see page 10). With a single 'ply' of yarn, work a straight st over centre of eye in a contrasting colour (white or green).

Above: *Pumpkin and Cat*

CHRISTMAS IN TOYTOWN

It's Christmas Eve and Sam the Snowman looks on as Santa and Rudolf deliver presents to the children in Toytown – Soldier, Clown, Bear, Little Girl and Little Boy.

MATERIALS FOR FATHER CHRISTMAS

- Double knitting yarn: 40 g pink for hands and head, 100 g red for clothes, 40 g white for beard and trim, 25 g black for boots, 40 g brown for belt and sack
- Small amount of double knitting yarn in yellow for buckle
- Pair of 3¼ mm (old size 10) knitting needles *or size to obtain correct tension*
- Good quality washable stuffing
- Red pencil for cheeks

FATHER CHRISTMAS

SIZE Father Christmas measures approx 33 cm (13 in) in height (including hat), when worked in recommended tension

TENSION 27 sts and 38 rows to 10 cm (4 in) measured over st st and worked on 3¼ mm needles
   Check your tension before beginning and change needle size if necessary.

DOLL

LEGS, BODY AND HEAD
The 2 legs are worked separately and then joined at the top.

RIGHT LEG
*With black (for boots), cast on 24 sts.
1st row (RS) K into front and back of each st. (48 sts)
Starting with a P row, work 13 rows in st st, so ending with a P row.*
Next row (RS) K6, (K3tog) 9 times, K15. (30 sts)
**Starting with a P row, work 11 rows in st st, so ending with a P row.
Break off black and change to red for top of leg (and body).
Starting with a K row, work 20 rows in st st, so ending with a P row.**
Break off yarn and slip sts onto a spare needle. This completes right leg.

LEFT LEG
Work as for right leg from * to *.
Next row (RS) K15, (K3tog) 9 times, K6. (30 sts)
Complete as for right leg from ** to **, but do not break off yarn.

JOINING LEGS

With RS facing, K30 sts of left leg, then K30 sts of right leg from spare needle. (60 sts)
Starting with a P row, work 31 rows in st st, so ending with a P row.

NECK SHAPING

Next row (RS) (K2tog) 30 times. (30 sts)
Break off red and change to pink for head.
P one row.
Next row K into front and back of each st. (60 sts)
Starting with a P row, work 29 rows in st st, so ending with a P row.
Next row (RS) (K2tog) 30 times. (30 sts)
Next row (P2tog) 15 times. (15 sts)
Break off yarn leaving a long loose end.
Using a blunt-ended needle, thread loose end through all 15 sts on needle, pull yarn to gather tightly, then fasten off.

ARMS (make 2)

With red, cast on 12 sts.
1st row (RS) K into front and back of first st, K to last st, K into front and back of last st.
2nd row P to end.
Rep last 2 rows 6 times more. (26 sts)
Starting with a K row, work 12 rows in st st, so ending with a P row.
Break off red and change to pink for hand.
Starting with a K row, work 10 rows in st st, so ending with a P row.
Next row (RS) (K2tog) 13 times. (13 sts)
Break off yarn leaving a long loose end and fasten off as for top of head.

NOSE

With pink, cast on 4 sts.
1st row K into front and back of each st. (8 sts)
Starting with a P row, work 7 rows in st st, so ending with a P row.
Next row (RS) (K2tog) 4 times. (4 sts)
Break off yarn leaving a long loose end and fasten off as for top of head.

BEARD

With white, cast on 18 sts.
K one row.
Next row K into front and back of first st, K to last st, K into front and back of last st.
Rep last row 10 times more. (40 sts)
K 9 rows.
Next row K6, turn leaving rem sts on a spare needle to be used later.

Working on first side of beard only, K 20 rows. Cast off.
Return to rem st on spare needle, rejoin yarn and cast off 28 centre sts, K to end. (6 sts)
K 20 rows. Cast off.

FINISHING

Finish and stuff body, head and legs as for Old Woman in Shoe (see page 106).
Arms Finish arms and sew to body as for Wendy Witch (see page 128).
Beard Sew inner edge of beard to head so that horizontal edge is 3.5 cm (1¼ in) from neck.
Nose Oversew all along outer edge of nose and pull to gather slightly. Stuff nose lightly and pull up gathers tightly. Sew nose to head just above horizontal edge of beard.
Embroidery Using a single 'ply' of red yarn and working in backstitch, work a semi-circle for the mouth (just below nose on beard).
Using black yarn, embroider eyes (see instructions on page 10).
Colour cheeks and nose with red pencil.

COAT AND BOOTS

COAT BOTTOM

With white, cast on 90 sts.
K 3 rows (garter st).
Break off white and change to red.
Starting with a K row, work 12 rows in st st, so ending with a P row.
Break off red and change to brown for belt.
K 2 rows.
Starting with a K row, work 4 rows in st st, so ending with a P row.
P one row.
Cast off purlwise.

SLEEVE CUFFS (make 2)

With white, cast on 35 sts.
K 4 rows (garter st).
Cast off.

BOOT TOPS (make 2)

With white, cast on 50 sts.
K 4 rows (garter st).
Cast off.

FINISHING

Coat bottom Join centre back seam (row ends) of coat bottom. Turn right side out. Put coat

Father Christmas

bottom on doll and sew cast-off edge to waist about 6 cm (2¼ in) below neck.

With yellow yarn, work a buttonhole stitch buckle on belt.

Sleeve cuffs Join row ends of cuffs. Slip cuffs onto arms and position so that cuff overlaps hand and sleeve. Sew each cuff in place round both cast-off and cast-on edge.

Boot tops Put each boot top round top of boot and join row ends. Sew cast-on and cast-off edges to leg and top of boot.

HAT

TO MAKE

With white, cast on 90 sts.

K 5 rows (garter st).

Break off white and change to red.

Starting with a K row, work 4 rows in st st, so ending with a P row.

Next row (RS) *K8, K2tog, rep from * to end. (81 sts)

Starting with a P row, work 4 rows in st st, so ending with a K row.

Next row (WS) *P7, P2tog, rep from * to end. (72 sts)

Starting with a K row, work 4 rows in st st.

Next row *K6, K2tog, rep from * to end. (63 sts)

Starting with a P row, work 4 rows in st st.

Next row *P5, P2tog, rep from * to end. (54 sts)

Starting with a K row, work 4 rows in st st.

Next row (RS) *K4, K2tog, rep from * to end. (45 sts)

Starting with a P row, work 4 rows in st st.

Next row *P3, P2tog, rep from * to end. (36 sts)

Starting with a K row, work 4 rows in st st.

Next row (RS) *K2, K2tog, rep from * to end. (27 sts)

Starting with a P row, work 4 rows in st st.

Next row *P1, P2tog, rep from * to end. (18 sts)

Starting with a K row, work 4 rows in st st.

Next row (RS) (K2tog) 9 times. (9 sts)

Starting with a P row, work 4 rows in st st.

Break off yarn leaving a long loose end.

Using a blunt-ended needle, thread loose end through all 9 sts on needle, pull yarn to gather tightly, then fasten off.

FINISHING

With right sides tog, join hat seam (row ends). Turn right side out and stuff pointed top lightly. Sew hat to top of head along cast-on edge.

With white, make a pompon (see instructions on pages 11-12) 4 cm (1½ in) in diameter and sew to top of hat.

Fold down top of hat and stitch in place.

SACK

TO MAKE

With brown, cast on 81 sts.

Starting with a K row, work 48 rows in st st, so ending with a P row.

Next row (RS) K1, *yfwd, K2tog, rep from * to end. (81 sts)

K 4 rows (garter st).

Cast off.

FINISHING

Fold sack in half with right sides tog, then join row ends tog and cast-on edge tog. Turn right side out.

Using brown yarn, make a twisted cord 48 cm (19 in) long (see instructions on page 13 for how to make a twisted cord).

Starting at side seam, thread finished cord through eyelet holes at top of sack. Tie ends of cord tog.

MATERIALS FOR RUDOLF

- Double knitting yarn: 100 g brown and small amounts in black for eyes, red for nose and dark brown for antlers
- Pair of 3¼ mm (old size 10) knitting needles *or size to obtain correct tension*
- Good quality washable stuffing
- Two plastic drinking straws 5 mm (³⁄₁₆ in) in diameter for antlers

RUDOLF THE RED NOSED REINDEER

SIZE Rudolf measures approx 27 cm (10½ in) in height (including antlers), when worked in recommended tension

TENSION As for Father Christmas

BODY AND LEGS

With brown, cast on 67 sts.
Rudolf is begun at top of back legs as follows:
1st row (RS) K25, (K into front and back of next st) 17 times, K25. (84 sts)
Starting with a P row, work 13 rows in st st.
Next row (RS) Cast off 25 sts, K to end. (59 sts)
Next row Cast off 25 sts, P to end. (34 sts)
BACK
Starting with a K row, work 34 rows in st st, so ending with a P row.
FRONT LEGS
Next row (RS) Cast on 25 sts, K to end. (59 sts)
Next row Cast off 25 sts, P to end. (84 sts)

Rudolf the Red Nosed Reindeer

Starting with a K row, work 13 rows in st st, so ending with a K row.
Next row (WS) P25, (P2tog) 17 times, P25. (67 sts)
Next row K25, (K2tog) 8 times, K26. (59 sts)
Starting with a P row, work 13 rows in st st, so ending with a P row.
Next row (RS) Cast off 25 sts, K to end. (34 sts)
Next row Cast off 25 sts, P to end. (9 sts)
STOMACH
Starting with a K row, work 34 rows in st st, so ending with a P row.
BACK LEGS
Next row (RS) Cast on 25 sts, K to end. (34 sts)
Next row Cast on 25 sts, P to end. (59 sts)
Starting with a K row, work 14 rows in st st.
Cast off.

HEAD

With brown, cast on 14 sts.
Starting with a K row, work 2 rows in st st, so ending with a P row.
*****Next row** (RS) K into front and back of first st, K to last st, K into front and back of last st.
P one row.*
Rep from * to * 5 times more. (26 sts)
Starting with a K row, work 32 rows in st st, so ending with a P row.
******Next row** (RS) K2tog, K to last 2 sts, K2tog.
P one row.**
Rep from ** to ** 5 times more. (14 sts)
Starting with a K row, work 2 rows in st st.
Cast off.

EARS (make 2)

With brown, cast on 6 sts.
1st row (RS) K into front and back of each st. (12 sts)
Starting with a P row, work 9 rows in st st, so ending with a P row.
Next row (RS) (K2tog) 6 times. (6 sts)
Break off yarn leaving a long loose end.
Using a blunt-ended needle, thread loose end through all 6 sts on needle, pull yarn to gather tightly, then fasten off.

LONG ANTLER PIECES (make 2)

With dark brown, cast on 6 sts.
Starting with a K row, work 28 rows in st st.
Cast off.

SHORT ANTLER PIECES (make 4)

With dark brown, cast on 6 sts.

Starting with a K row, work 14 rows in st st. Cast off.

NOSE

Make nose as for Father Christmas (see page 134), but use red instead of pink.

TAIL

With brown, cast on 8 sts.
Starting with a K row, work 10 rows in st st, so ending with a P row.
Next row (RS) (K2tog) 4 times. (4 sts)
Break off yarn leaving a long loose end and fasten off as for ears.

FINISHING

Body and legs With right sides tog, join first cast-on edge of back legs to last cast-off edge of back legs. Leaving an opening along stomach for turning and stuffing, join remaining cast-on and cast-off edges of each leg and join row ends of stomach to row ends of back. Turn right side out.

Stuff each leg very firmly (so that reindeer will stand up), then stuff body firmly. Sew opening on stomach tog.

Head With right sides tog, join tog cast-on and cast-off edges of head, then join row ends, leaving an opening for turning and stuffing. Turn right side out.

Stuff head and sew opening tog. Sew back of head to body.

Antlers Cut two 7 cm (2¾ in) lengths of drinking straw and four 4 cm (1½ in) lengths. With wrong side facing straw, wrap a long antler piece around each of two longer straws. Sew row ends of each antler tog around straw, then over-sew top and bottom of antler tog. Using four shorter straws, make four short antlers in same way. Sew two short antlers to each long antler piece, the first 4 cm (1½ in) down from top and the other 6 cm (2¼ in) down from top. Sew completed antlers to centre of top of head about 1 cm (⅜ in) apart.

Ears With wrong sides tog, join row ends of each ear. Do not stuff. Join cast-on edge of each ear tog, keeping seam at side of ear. Sew each ear to top of head about 1 cm (¼ in) below antlers and about 4 cm (1½ in) apart.

Nose Stuff and gather as for Father Christmas (see page 134). Sew nose to head 2 cm (¾ in) up for lower edge of head.

Embroidery Using black yarn, embroider eyes (see page 10).

Tail With wrong sides tog, join row ends of tail, leaving cast-on edge open. Stuff tail lightly and sew open end to back of reindeer.

MATERIALS FOR TOYTOWN KIDS

- Double knitting yarn: 50 g in pink for heads, hands and legs, 25 g black for shoes
- Small amounts of double knitting yarn in red, white, light green, mid-blue, yellow, orange, brown, light brown, green, pale lilac and purple
- Pair of 3¼ mm (old size 10) knitting needles *or size to obtain correct tension*
- Good quality washable stuffing
- Red pencil for cheeks

TOYTOWN KIDS

SIZE The Toytown Kids measure approx 15.5 cm (6 in) in height, when worked in recommended tension

TENSION As for Father Christmas

LITTLE GIRL

BASIC DOLL

Work arms, legs, body and head as for Girls of Old Woman in Shoe (see the instructions given on page 108), using pale lilac yarn for body colour.

SKIRT

Work skirt as for Girls' skirts (see page 109), using purple yarn and omitting contrasting coloured stripe after hem.

FINISHING

Finish and stuff legs, body, head and arms as for Old Woman in Shoe (see the instructions given on page 106).

Make plaited hair with fringe, finish skirt and work features as for Girls (see pages 108-110). Colour cheeks with red pencil.

LITTLE BOY

BASIC DOLL

Work arms, legs, body and head as for Little Girl, using white for body colour.

TROUSERS

Work trousers as for Boys' trousers (see pages 110-111), using mid-blue.

HAT

Make bicolour hat as given for Girls' hats (see

page 109), using red for the first colour and yellow for the second colour.

KNITTED HAIR
With brown, cast on 30 sts.
Starting with a K row, work 6 rows in st st.
Cast off.

FINISHING
Finish and stuff legs, body, head and arms as for Little Girl.

With rev st st side of hair as right side, sew knitted hair to head with row ends at sides of face. Then finish hat as for Girls' hats (page 110) and sew to head so that lower edge of hat covers top edge of hair.

Finish trousers and work features as for Boys (see page 111). Colour cheeks with red pencil.

SOLDIER

BASIC DOLL
Work arms, legs, body and head as for Little Girl, using red for body colour.

TROUSERS
The 2 legs of the trousers are worked separately and then joined at the top.
FIRST LEG
*With black, cast on 20 sts.
K 2 rows (garter st).
Starting with a P row, work 9 rows in st st, so ending with a P row.*
Break off yarn and slip sts onto a spare needle. This completes first leg.
SECOND LEG
Rep from * to * for second leg. Do not break off yarn.
JOINING LEGS
With RS facing, K20 sts of second leg, then K20 sts of first leg from spare needle. (40 sts)
Starting with a P row, work 4 rows in st st, so ending with a K row.
Break off black and change to red.
P 3 rows.
K one row.
Break off red and change to white for belt.
P one row. Cast off purlwise.

HAT
With black, cast on 30 sts.
K 2 rows (garter st).

Starting with a P row, work 11 rows in st st, so ending with a P row.
Next row (RS) (K2tog) 15 times. (15 sts)
Break off yarn leaving a long loose end.
Using a blunt-ended needle, thread loose end through all 15 sts on needle, pull yarn to gather tightly, then fasten off.

FINISHING
Finish and stuff legs, body, head and arms as for Little Girl.
Hat Join centre back seam (row ends) of hat. Turn right side out. Sew hat to top of head.

For chin strap, secure two strands of yellow yarn under hat at 'ear' and secure other ends of these two strands under hat at other 'ear' so that strands pass under chin. Then using yellow yarn, work buttonhole stitch around this doubled yarn from ear to ear.
Hair For hair work a few loops of brown yarn to stick out from under hat at centre of forehead.

Finish trousers and work facial features as for Little Boy.

With yellow yarn, work a buttonhole stitch buckle on belt (see page 40). Using black yarn, embroider two short (doubled) horizontal sts below neck down chest for 'buttons'.

BEAR

BASIC DOLL
Work legs, body and head as for Little Girl, using yellow for body colour, but using light brown instead of black for feet and instead of pink for legs and head, and working in st st throughout.
Work arms as for Little Girl, using yellow for sleeve and light brown for hand.

TROUSERS
Work trousers as for Little Boy, using green.

EARS (make 2)
With light brown, cast on 8 sts.
1st row (RS) K into front and back of each st. (16 sts)
Starting with a P row, work 3 rows in st st. Cast off.

FINISHING
Finish and stuff legs, body, head and arms as for Old Woman in Shoe (see page 106).

Ears Join ear seams (row ends) with wrong sides tog and oversew cast-on edges tog, keeping seams at centre. Do not stuff. Sew ears to top of head.

Finish trousers as for Little Boy.

Embroidery Using a single 'ply' of black yarn and working in satin st, make a triangle for the nose. Still using black, work a vertical straight st from tip of nose to centre of mouth, then work a V-shaped mouth.

Using black, embroider eyes (see page 10).

CLOWN

BASIC DOLL

Work arms, legs, body and head as for Little Girl, but when body colour is called for, work in stripes of 2 rows orange and 2 rows yellow.

TROUSERS

The 2 legs of the trousers are worked separately and then joined at the top.

FIRST LEG

**With red, cast on 20 sts.

K one row.

Next row (RS) *K1, K into front and back of next st, rep from * to end. (30 sts)

Starting with a P row, work 9 rows in st st, so ending with a P row.**

Break off yarn and slip sts onto a spare needle. This completes first leg.

SECOND LEG

Rep from ** to ** for second leg. Do not break off yarn.

JOINING LEGS

With RS facing, K30 sts of second leg, then K30 sts of first leg from spare needle. (60 sts)

Starting with a P row, work 8 rows in st st, so ending with a K row.

Next row (WS) *K1, K2tog, rep from * to end. (40 sts)

Cast off.

HAT

Work hat as for Soldier, but using mid-blue instead of black.

FINISHING

Finish and stuff legs, body, head and arms as for Little Girl.

Hair Cut thirty 11 cm (4¼ in) lengths of light green yarn. Using a matching length of yarn tie strands tog at centre. Brush strands with a hair brush to fluff hair. Sew tied section of hair to top of head and spread hair out over top of head. Part hair to either side of face and sew hat to top of head.

Make a bow with a single strand of white yarn and sew bow to front of hat a little to the side, half way from the top and bottom of hat.

Finish trousers and work features as for Little Boy, but make mouth and nose bigger.

MATERIALS FOR SAM THE SNOWMAN

- Double knitting yarn: 125 g white for arms, legs, body and head, 40 g red for jacket, 25 g black for hat
- Small amounts of double knitting yarn in yellow and green for scarf
- Pair of 3¼ mm (old size 10) knitting needles or size to obtain correct tension
- Good quality washable stuffing
- Red pencil for cheeks

SAM THE SNOWMAN

SIZE Sam the Snowman measures approx 31 cm (12¼ in) in height (including hat), when worked in recommended tension

TENSION As for Father Christmas

DOLL

LEGS, BODY AND HEAD
Work as for legs, body and head of Father Christmas (see pages 132-134), but use white

ARMS
Work as for Father Christmas (see page 134), but using white throughout.

FINISHING
Finish and stuff body, head and legs as for Old Woman in Shoe (see page 106).
Arms Finish arms and sew to body as for Wendy Witch (see page 128).
Embroidery Using a single 'ply' of red yarn and working in backstitch, work a semi-circle for Sam the Snowman's mouth.
   Using a single 'ply' of red yarn, work a short horizontal straight st and work twice over same st for nose.
   Using black yarn, embroider eyes (see instructions on page 10).
   Colour cheeks with red pencil.

JACKET

SLEEVES (make 2)
With red, cast on 42 sts.
K 2 rows (garter st).
Starting with a P row, work 9 rows in st st, so ending with a P row.
Next row (RS) Cast off 3 sts, K to end. (39 sts)
Next row Cast off 3 sts, P to end. (36 sts)
*Next row K2, K2tog, K to last 4 sts, K2tog tbl, K2.
P one row.*
Rep from * to * 7 times more. (20 sts)
Break off yarn and leave sts on a st holder.
Make a second sleeve in the same way.

BACK
With red, cast on 49 sts.

K 2 rows (garter st).
Starting with a P row, work 7 rows in st st, so ending with a P row.
Next row (RS) Cast off 3 sts, K to end. (46 sts)
Next row Cast off 3 sts, P to end. (43 sts)
*Next row K2, K2tog, K to last 4 sts, K2tog tbl, K2.
P one row.*
Rep from * to * 7 times more. (27 sts)
Break off yarn and leave sts on a st holder.

LEFT FRONT
With red, cast on 17 sts.
K 2 rows (garter st).
*Next row (WS) K2, P15.
K one row.*
Rep from * to * twice more.
Next row K2, P15.
Next row (RS) Cast off 3 sts, K to end. (14 sts)
Next row K2, P to end.
**Next row K2, K2tog, K to end.
Next row K2, P to end.**
Rep from ** to ** 7 times more. (6 sts)
Break off yarn and leave sts on a st holder.

RIGHT FRONT
With red, cast on 17 sts.
K 2 rows (garter st).
*Next row (WS) P15, K2.
K one row.*
Rep from * to * 3 times more.
Next row (RS) Cast off 3 sts, P to last 2 sts, K2. (14 sts)
**Next row K to last 4 sts, K2tog tbl, K2.
Next row P to last 2 sts, K2.**
Rep from ** to ** 7 times more. (6 sts)
Do not break off yarn.

NECKBAND
With red and with RS facing, work across 6 sts of right front, 20 sts of first sleeve, 27 sts of back, 20 sts of second sleeve and 6 sts of left front in that order as follows:
*K1, K2tog, rep from * to last st, K1. (53 sts)
K one row.
Cast off.

FINISHING
Join raglan sleeve seams of jacket sewing sides of shaped tops of sleeves to sides of shaped tops of fronts and back. Then join sleeve and side seams. Turn jacket right side out and put on Sam the Snowman.

HAT

TO MAKE

Make hat, stuff and sew to top of head as for hat for Daddy Octopus (see page 121).

SCARF

TO MAKE

With yellow, cast on 10 sts.

*K 2 rows yellow.
K 2 rows green.*
Rep from * to * until scarf measures 36 cm (14 in) from cast-on edge, ending with 2 rows yellow.
Cast off.

FINISHING

Using yellow and green alternately, make fringe along short ends of scarf.

Tie scarf round Sam the Snowman's neck.

Below: *Sam the Snowman*

INDEX